C000051063

Psychosis is one of a series
of low-cost books under the
title **PSYCHOANALYTIC ideas,**
which brings together the best
of Public Lectures given by
analysts of the British Psycho-
Analytical Society on important
psychoanalytic subjects.
The books can be ordered from
the Society's web site
http://www.psychoanalysis.org.uk/psideas.html
or by calling the PSYCHOANALYTIC
ideas 24-hour sales line
+44 (0) 207 722 2707

Series Editors
Inge Wise and Paul Williams

Psychosis (madness)

Edited by Paul Williams

The Institute of Psycho-Analysis, London

Institute of Psycho-Analysis
Byron House
112a Shirland Road
London W9 2EQ

http://www.psychoanalysis.org.uk

ISBN 0 9537105 0 5

First published 1999
Papers © 1999 the authors
This compilation © 1999 Institute of Psycho-Analysis, London

Revised printing with corrections 2001

A CIP catalogue record for this book is available from
the British Library

Designed & typeset in Meta and Swift by Phil Baines

Printed in England

Acknowledgements

I wish to thank all those whose ideas and efforts have contributed to *Psychoanalytic Ideas*: Dr Mike Conran, who first suggested publishing several Public Lectures in book form; Dr Elizabeth Spillius PhD, Professor Peter Fonagy PhD, FBA, and all other members of the Publication Committee; Dr Martin Edwards for copy-editing; Rosalind Oliver for proofreading; Phil Baines for his design and enthusiasm; Linda Carter-Jackson and Lyndsay MacDonald for their administrative expertise; Nick Hall for his. My special thanks go to Professor Paul Williams, without whose great dedication and moral support this series would probably not have seen the light of day.

Quotations from Dennis Potter's *The Singing Detective* are reproduced by permission of Faber & Faber Ltd.

Inge Wise, Series Editor

Paul Williams

Introduction

In 1994 my colleague Murray Jackson and I reported on the extent to which psychotic disorders bring tremendous suffering to victims and their relatives and constitute the heaviest burden on mental health services in the western world. The treatment situation for many of these patients has gradually deteriorated over the years in many countries, including in the UK (Jackson & Williams 1994). The provision of facilities and trained clinicians to work in adequate depth with such patients has been reduced as a consequence of economic pressures, despite a need for systematic research into and treatment of these disorders, for which no comprehensive cure is available.

Although much is known about psychotic disorders, many conjectures are still to be confirmed or refuted and a great deal remains to be understood. For example, the precise mode of action of biological methods of treatment has yet to be properly elucidated, and claims for psychoanalysis and its offspring, psychoanalytic psychotherapy, as an effective treatment for psychotic disorders have yet to be substantiated at the level of formal scientific proof. A further complicating factor is that whilst the definition of psychosis is generally agreed upon, the same cannot yet be said for schizophrenia, despite continuing research into its genetic, neurological and psychological aspects. Schizophrenia is regarded as a disorder, or group of disorders, within the broader category of psychotic conditions. It is characterised by the prominence of either negative or positive symptoms with associated tendencies towards passivity and withdrawal, and activity. Disorders of thought and perception prevail. The illness seems to arise on a basis of a predisposition, manifested as a vulnerability of biological or psychological origin, or both. It tends towards a chronic course, although recent studies have shown that the long-term outcome is better than has been believed, especially if attacks can be treated early (at or near the onset). The presence of structural brain abnormality in a large proportion of cases has been demonstrated by modern neuro-physiological research using non-invasive methods which permit direct observation of brain function (cf. Rubin *et al* 1993, McNeil *et al* 1993). Although the nature and origin of this abnormality are not fully clear, the suppression of positive symptoms such as hallucinations by anti-psychotic drugs during an acute attack is impressive. The view that schizophrenia is a neuro-developmental disorder of organic origin is based on research findings that are sound. However, the application of such findings as general truths about the nature and treatment requirements of schizophrenia can sometimes be quite misleading. Studies of brain pathology reveal statistical significance only, and the common disorders detected in the 'schizophrenic brain' are by no means confined to schizophrenia. It is not yet known how frequently such disorders occur, or how often they have pathological consequences for personality development and psychological functioning. Genetic studies of schizophrenia have proved to be more complex than many had imagined. The essential fact that genes represent tendencies, and thus may be modifiable by favourable early environmental conditions, has been demonstrated by studies which show that where a genetically predisposed infant is born into a secure and mature family the genetic effects may be neutralised (eg Tienari 1992a, 1992b). Lewontin, speaking of the 'doctrine of DNA', criticises the current tendency to over-emphasise the role of genetics in human development. He points out that 'genes affect how sensitive one is to the environment, and the environment affects how relevant one's genetic differences may be' (Lewontin 1993, p.30).

The term 'psychosis' encompasses a wide group of mental disorders which have in common a serious impairment of the individual's capacity to remain in contact with reality. They are often accompanied by confusion and disorders of thought and perception which can find expression as delusional thinking and hallucinatory experiences. The causes of an individual psychotic episode or of long-term vulnerability are to be sought in biological, social or psychological factors (or a combination of all three). Each of the disciplines which study these factors has its own language and method of investigation. Bridges, conceptual and operational, between the disciplines may be difficult, sometimes impossible, to construct. Yet each discipline is relevant, individually or in combination, to the acquisition of a deeper understanding of the nature and treatment of psychosis. The co-operation of different specialists is needed if the needs of the psychotic individual are to be met fully. It would seem that under such circumstances, it is reasonable to expect practitioners skilled in particular specialities or sub-specialities to acquire a level of general understanding of, or contact with, other disciplines to permit constructive debate to take place. In practice, co-operation appears, regrettably, to be the exception rather than the rule. This is particularly unfortunate as individuals suffering from psychosis tend to communicate three overriding needs to their carers: first, the need for asylum (care and protection); second, the need to reduce the pain and confusion created by their symptoms; and third, the need to talk to someone in order to try to find out what is going on inside them. The roles of the hospital or community care service, psychiatrist and psychoanalyst or psychotherapist are complementary, yet these services tend to work separately rather than together, at least in the United Kingdom. When these services do act in a co-ordinated way, the personal meaning of the patient's psychotic condition can be treated and explored. It is under these conditions that psychoanalytic thinking plays a central role in the treatment of psychosis.

Psychoanalysis offers a source of knowledge for the understanding and treatment of psychotic disorders, which helps those working with these patients in three ways. First, psychoanalysis helps to give coherent meaning to confusing or bizarre communications and this can be a relief to all concerned (by furthering understanding of the patient's preoccupations and problems, it also helps to reduce the risk of inappropriate behaviour by professional staff in treatment centres, towards the patient). Second, psychoanalytic concepts can act as a foundation for the formulation and implementation of treatment plans. A psychoanalytically informed perspective enables a variety of treatment modalities to be employed in a truly complementary manner. Individual psychotherapy, behavioural, cognitive, family, or group-analytic therapy, and psycho-pharmacological procedures may be appropriately used according to a patient's needs and capacities at a given point in treatment. Third, psychoanalytic ideas permit the selection of psychotic patients likely to benefit from long-term individual psychoanalytic psychotherapy, or formal psychoanalysis.

Psychoanalysis and its derivative method, psychoanalytic psychotherapy, have long proved themselves to be effective treatment methods when applied under the right conditions with the right patients. The effectiveness derives from the fact that psychoanalysis is a psychodynamic psychology: what distinguishes its theoretical system from others is its developmental perspective and fundamental concepts. These include the instinctual mental life, conscious and unconscious, developmental phases, conflicts and defences, internal (psychic) reality, the tendency to repeat the past in the present, the phenomena of transference, counter-transference and the dynamic working-through of pathogenic concepts during the course of treatment – these concepts constitute a psychoanalytic, or psychodynamic, theory and perspective. This perspective permits not only an explanation of the psychotic condition but also a search for the intra-psychic and subjective meaning of the mental events which are taking place. The consequence of such a search can be that the patient is offered the understanding he or she urgently needs.

In this volume we see how a number of British psychoanalysts (who are also psychiatrists) introduce us to psychoanalytic definitions of intra-psychic and subjective meaning in patients suffering psychotic conditions. Irrespective of the particular type of psychotic illness under consideration or the context of treatment, each paper illustrates how the psychoanalytic clinician searches to establish meaning from events which are highly complex and which can at times appear to be overwhelmingly confusing. Obviously, these pages cannot deal with all the theoretical and clinical implications of psychoanalytic thinking in relation to psychosis, as this is a vast subject. The Public Lectures given by the British Psycho-Analytical Society traditionally sought to demonstrate simply, yet without simple-mindedness, how psychoanalysts approach their subject, and these papers exemplify this tradition. The history of the Public Lecture series goes back many decades and the series has proved itself to be an effective way of introducing psychoanalytic ideas to an interested audience who are not necessarily psychoanalysts or psychotherapists. This particular selection of Public Lectures is designed to stimulate thinking about psychosis according to ways in which contemporary British psychoanalysts have developed their understanding of the condition, and to encourage further reading and exploration. Each author in this small volume has long experience of treating patients with psychosis, either in the British National Health Service or privately, or both, and these papers represent their work at its best. For those who wish to find out more about the psychoanalytic understanding of psychosis, a brief list of relevant publications is given below amongst the references to this introduction.

You will also notice that several of the authors in this book make mention of the role of the hospital in the psychiatric and psychoanalytic treatment of psychosis. Today, at the start of a new millenium, we live and work in an era when the role of the hospital as a source of asylum and treatment of mental illness can be seen to have diminished drastically. Whilst the anti-therapeutic aspects of mental hospitals have been well recognised, there are many clinicians and patients who feel that the demise of the hospital, as part of the embrace of community care, may have impoverished our care of the seriously disturbed. The opportunity for a period of rest and respite, for time away from what might be damaging social or family circumstances, for an opportunity to address 'full-time' the source of one's troubles – these are today much less available to patients suffering from psychotic illnesses. Community care has many advantages and benefits which are beyond dispute (if adequately funded), but we must not forget that the treatment of psychotic illness takes a great deal of time and effort, and that any sacrifice of the reality of this difficulty on the altar of efficiency is a betrayal of the suffering of these patients.

Psychoanalysts have a long and distinguished history of working within and alongside psychiatric institutions in many different ways to achieve a treatment regime which meets the needs of the individual psychotic patient. Perhaps the most recent example of this is the work in Scandinavia on what has been termed the 'need-adapted' approach to the treatment of schizophrenia. This makes sophisticated, co-ordinated use of hospital facilities, community care, out-patient treatment and individual, group and family treatments using psychoanalytic principles and methods in order to create a flexible and more precise response to the features and phases of the psychotic illness being treated (Alanen 1997). The success achieved through this multidisciplinary approach is convincing and impressive. Given an appropriate setting capable of managing the vicissitudes of psychotic illness, psychoanalytic treatment has demonstrated time and time again how the opportunity to discern, work through and integrate the meaning of psychotic thinking can have profound, durable therapeutic benefits. We hope that these papers offer a glimpse of how this process occurs.

References*

ALANEN, Y (1997) *Schizophrenia: need adapted treatment*, Karnac Books

ARIETI, S (1994) *Interpretation of Schizophrenia*, Jason Aronson: Northvale

ELLWOOD, J (ed.) (1995) *Psychosis: understanding and treatment*, Jessica Kingsley

JACKSON, M (1992) 'Learning to think about schizoid thinking', *Psychoanalytic Psychotherapy*, 6 (3), pp.191–203

JACKSON, M & WILLIAMS, P (1994) *Unimaginable Storms: a search for meaning in psychosis*, Karnac Books

LEWONTIN, R J (1993) *The Doctrine of DNA: biology and ideology*, Penguin

LIDZ, R W & LIDZ, T (1949) 'The family environment of schizophrenic patients', *American Journal of Psychiatry*, 106, pp.332–45

McNEIL, T F, CANTOR-GRACE, E, NORDSTROM, L G & ROSENLUND, T (1993) 'Head circumference in "pre-schizophrenic" and control neonates', *British Journal of Psychotherapy*, 162, pp.517–23

REY, J H (1994) *Universals of Psychoanalysis*, Free Association Books

ROSENFELD, H A (1975) *Psychotic States: a psycho-analytic approach*, Hogarth Press

RUBIN, P, KARLE, A, MOLLER-MADSEN, S et al (1993) 'Computerised tomography in newly diagnosed schizophrenic and schizophreniform disorder: a controlled blind study', *British Journal of Psychotherapy*, 163, pp.604–12

SEARLES, H A (1965) *Collected Papers on Schizophrenia and Related Subjects*, Hogarth Press

SEGAL, H (1991) *Dream, Phantasy & Art*, Routledge

TIENARI, P (1992a) 'Interaction between genetic vulnerability and family environment' in *Psychotherapy of Schizophrenia: facilitating and obstructive factors*, Oslo: University Press

— (1992b) 'Implications of adoption studies on schizophrenia', *British Journal of Psychotherapy* Supplement 18, pp.52–8

YORKE, C, WISEBERG, S & FREEMAN, T (1989) *Development and Psychopathology*, New Haven & London: Yale University Press

---

* Publishers cited in this book are London-based, unless indicated otherwise.

1

Leslie Sohn

Psychosis and violence

Previously, in another place, I presented a paper on unprovoked assaults, and discussed some patients, one of whom will appear in this paper. From that I wrote a paper which appeared in the *International Journal of Psychoanalysis* (Sohn 1995).

I want to take a further look at the patient I described in order to emphasise the relationship of his psychotic state to the events of violence which brought him to our attention. And then, in contrast, I want to talk about a young psychotic woman who never resorted to physical violence, although she had had delusional ideas of having murdered – or somebody having been murdered, or somebody having murdered somebody – and she felt that she'd seen the dead body. Then I want to talk about two other men; one a borderline case with almost delusional belief in his sanity, whose violence was solely directed unwittingly to his own mind and its contents, and to the mind of others who were exposed to him, and we were expected to believe implicitly in his conclusions. To do so, and to believe that, would mean that the listener's mind would have totally given up its own scepticism and independent thinking. In other words, that the listener's mind would have felt murdered, or dead. This man deigned physical assault; he was above it, and I think he even deigned physical contact as well.

Originally this paper had a double title, and it had derived from a man called Mr M B. During our first meeting, Mr M B said to me: 'If the bloody black and white dog hadn't crossed the road at that moment, the police would never have thought of me. Anyway,' Mr M B then said, 'I didn't do what they said I did.' In fact he had violently attacked a man whom he thought he knew. He could never have done what the police thought that he had done. He had merely acted quite normally and acceptably. On the ward, Mr M B had threatened frequently to attack a fair-haired young man who was a fellow patient, for what he, Mr M B, thought were perfectly validly reasons. The fair-haired man, he believed, laughed and mocked him. He had no idea why the young man behaved in such a provocative way. Mr M B was not fair-haired: he was dark and swarthy, the son of a South American black man and European white woman. As I got to know more about Mr M B this question of his black and white origins arose in our meetings. He was ashamed of his mother and hated her for being with a black man who later had abandoned the family. He was similarly ashamed and hated his father for spoiling his own pedigree, and diluting his blackness. Mr M B's blackness and whiteness had dogged most of his 24 years.

The telling of these clinical moments leaves out the diagnosis. Mr M B was a paranoid schizophrenic, and experienced mental and environmental events according to the pattern laid down by his illness. He did not connect in any way the facts I've related to his attack on his victim: he was totally involved in the conviction that he held about the little black and white dog that had led the police to his door. The attack on the victim was seen by many who knew the victim and our patient. Mr M B not only wanted things to be either black or white, but he had simplified them in a strange story which explained everything to him. For Mr M B, a psychotic man, external reality is treated as if it were internal reality – something that can be manipulated at will. Internal reality itself is treated as though it consisted of simple, unalterable facts about the world. For Mr M B the dog might be described as the substantive noun of the present participles of his mind: thus it explained everything, as did the condensation of the thought represented by the black and white dog. He could tell me historical facts about his life and its contents, about his violent father, and facts about his mother: in fact, facts about his mother invaded his thoughts and his life. I could sense that they were significant to the genesis of his illness and its outcome, which had made him a particularly dangerous man, in my view. He, however, was detached from a capacity for mental continuity, and free of the significance of the facts he recounted. A condensed, literal version of his mind's hatreds operated in the black and white fashion I have outlined. Our patient would like to be the other young man on the ward – fair, or white, or pure – or, in contrast to this – black. In the short time I knew him, 'fair' seemed to signify the antithesis of the total unfairness of life that he had been dealt out. All these facts were waiting for a psychoanalyst to interpret to Mr M B.

However, if Mr M B had said, 'Right, Doctor, all that's very true. In the first place, I hated the facts of my parents' sexual relations; I hated it even more when I was old enough to know I would feel a mongrel amongst mongrels; my mother's post-natal long-term depression was equally disturbing to me; but tell me, dear Doctor: why couldn't I, why didn't I deal with all these facts and their repercussions in a mature way, so that I would know my story – its vicissitudes, its dangers – instead of my being desperately concerned with these fragmented versions of my mind's contents? Why is my mother's whiteness, which was not visited on me, so important? Or my idealised version of my father's blackness – why do I have such difficulty in tolerating mixed thoughts and feelings? And why do I simply corral my history into this black and white dog business? Why do I do it so violently, and why do I try to evacuate my unconscious totality into that nice white boy on the ward?' Mr M B never asked me these questions. He moved to safer territory. So I was left thinking I knew so much about him, and he knew so very little about himself. It's a classical forensic psychiatric phenomenon, wherein exists a major discrepancy between what the psychiatrist knows and what the patient knows, or rather doesn't know.

I'll try to answer Mr M B's unasked questions by talking about one of a group of patients all of whom possess a similar pattern of behaviour for similar reasons. This may create the possibility of explaining things to Mr M B when an opportunity arises, and it may explain why Mr M B didn't ever say to himself, 'What is there about me that makes me the way I am? Firstly, why do I never ask myself such a question? Why does my mind operate in this peculiar way, so as to avoid original causes and effects, and present me with strange thoughtless quandaries? For instance, do I ever actually stop to think, or do I replace thought with shallow, ready-made ideas?' The group of patients to which I refer and from which Mr M B comes (there are nine patients in the group in total) were all seen at the Dennis Hill Unit at the Bethlem Hospital, which is part of the joint Maudsley-Bethlem Hospital. I shall concentrate on one patient only and discuss him; as it turned out I could discuss any one of this small group as there is such a definitive similarity in them regarding their illnesses and behaviours. My original approach to these patients was to further an enquiry into their suitability for psychotherapy on the in-patient unit. Gradually, however, they became of interest as part of a more general investigation into their illness, and the particular patient to be reported upon was treated by myself.

The initial presentation of all these patients was a keen wish to speak and to be spoken to, but not necessarily to be spoken about. Gradually, a life-long mental illness manifested itself, and this induced truancy and a general unwillingness to attend sessions. Mostly there seemed to be a lack of interest in their own, sane selves. I think that their initial enthusiasm represented a vain hope to fully regain and re-establish their delusional objects, felt to be possibly lost as a result of finding themselves in a new hospital treatment system. From the outset one of the men (I will call him Mr J P) permitted us, by the nature of his referral, to formulate a long-term view of this man's treatment. There were no limitations on time regarding his treatment or length of admission. His future was intimately related to long-term treatment, and I was conscious throughout of the fact that, should there be any untoward developments in his illness and therefore in the therapy, I could rely on a full back-up system for further in-patient care on the unit. Another factor was Mr J P's capacity to be interested in and to maintain, to the best of his ability, his interest in being my patient.

We met regularly over a three-year period. The best of his ability included the vicissitudes of his capacity to act out. A minor version of this was physical illness, clearly attributable to excessive smoking and which with minor short intermissions stayed excessively dangerous, and on a few occasions he was cared for in bed. His sessions were inter-fered with as a result of acting out on two occasions, once for a period of a fortnight. Generally he dealt with this with a cheerful, manic, carefree smile. Far more serious were episodes of excessive drinking, and I am sure that on a few occasions he smoked cannabis. All these facts may point to a view that one could not call this a truly psychoana-lytic setting, whatever that means. A further complication was that, by the very nature of their treatment in a medium secure unit, all these patients were under varying categories of certification, and they were clearly told at the onset of their seeing me, that they could expect confidentiality, unless there was breach of security. Our contractual relationship would allow me to notify the unit authorities if such a breach occurred. Fortunately, this never had to take place.

By the time I saw Mr J P he was a 60-year-old, worn-out man. He'd been an in-patient in a secure special hospital for 15 years, having been admitted under Section in the late 1970s. He was emphysematous, and he smoked heavily. Until he got used to the possibility in his sessions that he could speak to me in an ordinary fashion, he spoke in an ordered, sycophantic, apologetic way, as if I were a pompous superior officer who not only demanded this but would punish him if he did not address me in this way. He would agree with everything I said to him, as if disagreement were highly dangerous. He'd waited a very long time to come to the Dennis Hill Unit, and this was the only means available to him to ensure treatment and to restore balance in his unbalanced mind. He would interlard his ideas, occasionally at the outset but more frequently later, with statements from literary and dramatic sources, and was clearly well read and informed. He claimed an attachment to racist political thoughts, and to Roman Catholicism. He certainly had a history of racist attitudes, and was occasionally overtly racist and superior. He'd grown up in the north of England, the fourth and youngest child in a coal-mining family. His father, a heavy drinking man, was described by the patient as having no status in the mining community. The patient, who himself worked underground for a year, failed to stay in his community and ran away from home at 16 to join a circus. Later, he went into the Guards, following one of his older brothers. His good record in the Guards was periodically spoilt by drinking bouts, but he finished his service despite a long period in detention. Various occupations, interests and wanderings followed. There are constant reports in his various hospital notes that he was felt to be rather a good journalist or a good actor, but invariably something would always interfere with and spoil the situation. The first admis-sion took place in his late twenties followed by a series of subsequent admissions, most of which were terminated by apparent cures, promises to stop drinking, and promises of refusal to take drugs. He was frequently discharged because of aggressive, destructive behaviour and some violence towards the staff.

Throughout all this, the diagnoses were all the standard ones of schizophrenia. But there were phases when he read, worked well, and even published short stories and literary criticism, and some poems. But he never seemed able to attach himself to anybody or anything for very long. He was married twice; both women left him. He was promiscuous, and there was a history of homosexual prostitution; not quite the sort of case that gets taken on at the Institute of Psychoanalysis! His story about the index offence varied in two essential details – firstly regarding the preface. He originally told me that his welfare benefits were a day late in arriving, which worried him. Later he corrected this. He had arrived at the DHSS office a day late because he'd been drinking heavily, and he'd expected that the nice lady at the office would be helpful, because she'd always been nice to him. She was unable to help him, however, and asked him to return later, but expressed doubts as to whether his benefits would be available. This doubt transmitted itself forcefully to him, reaching a climax on the platform of the tube station where he was going to take the train home. He stuck to this version of the story throughout his time with me. Somebody (ostensibly, the nice lady) who had been so helpful and kind was giving up on him, but it was his own fault. He was angry, excited, miserable and penniless. During his wait for the train home at the tube station he had grabbed a man – a total stranger – and pushed him forcibly towards the line. Fortunately, though the man's legs ended up dangling over the edge, he was saved from ghastly injury.

This is where the second change in the patient's story occurred, and this fact is interesting in the light of my ideas about such patients. Our patient behaved in telling me his story as if he were utterly convinced that the man he pushed was trying to commit suicide. He remembered this in his sessions with me, and admitted that he had great difficulty in giving up this belief. He added in this context that his own behaviour was merely to frighten the man out of committing suicide. In the later version of the story, he said the man had insulted him by calling him a Jew, and this had upset him. Actually, the two stories, though in a physical sense so far removed from each other, are not so dissimilar on close examination. In the first instance, he clearly projects his murderously suicidal ideas into the man; by trying to frighten him he is also indicating how he split the conflict that existed in the psychotic part of his mind. We also know, in the second instance, about our patient's racist attitudes. Jews were not very much higher in his social map than 'niggers'. Here, once again, in his picture of himself at the time of the offence, is a depressing disparity between a despised figure and his mind's idealised view of himself. After the attack, his behaviour was described as grandiose. He claimed to have won the VC and seems to have justified himself by making racist comments about Jews and black people.

In my description of what I believe to be his psychopathology, we are looking at events taking place in the psychotic part of the mind of this man; so that if I say that he feels himself to be inferior to the person he was before the traumatic disappointment in the welfare office, this is a way of using ordinary language to describe the workings of the psychotic part of his mind. In him, such a feeling is furnished not only by the character defects of a racist, but also with the added exaggerations of maniacal superiority that a psychotic mind can produce. Projections are split off violently and suddenly, and carry the need for delusional certainty. His good object, exemplified externally by the lady in the office, is but a protective veneer against his mind's adherence to delusional objects. She might be considered a possible symbol of his mind's delusional objects with which he communes and ruminates. Thus the total imagery of his psychotic mind, at that moment, is unaffected by any mitigating sanity, so that the feeling of murderousness to the nice lady has to be got rid of extremely quickly, if only to protect his own mental contents. When he feels inferior, he feels it as if he were an inferior Jew or black man, or combination of both. He successfully rids himself of such identifications, and this is confirmed by the material when he said he was accused of being a Jew, or that the man was suicidal. Our patient was merely 'trying to frighten' him. This is related to the projection of psychotic anxieties engendered by the events. But the question arises, however, once he's achieved a relatively bland, hypocritical position vis-à-vis his victim, why isn't it enough to enable him to walk away smugly, feeling all is aright with his mental world – thank you very much? After all, this sort of thing must have happened to him many times before. It could be seen, for example in his continuing to smoke despite his crippling emphysema, over which he triumphs, and not only by denying it, but by treating it as a statement of inferiority in somebody else. He spent much time persecuting his emphysema. But this time it's different. His mind is about to lose its feeling of having good, albeit delusional, objects within itself. And he can't project that feeling as he did the others without the physical enactment of reassurance. Later I'll discuss my view of how this happened.

Mr J P experienced a sense of grandiosity after the events I described above. This featured in two of the others belonging to this small in-patient group and is connected to the experience of loss. Loss, and the various responses and results of it, featured in Mr J P's sessions with me. In an indirect fashion he could talk about what was, what had been, what could have been, what so-and-so said or wrote and said or wrote no more. He seemed always to be protected from actual experiences of loss by a veneer of superiority, which in his everyday dealings on the unit irritated some people. He read and he discussed what he read, and wrote for the hospital magazine perfectly readable material. Gradually, statements about his childhood entered into the sessions. He could not understand why everyone made such a fuss of the failure of his family to be in touch with him, and he with them. It was a simple continuation of his childhood experiences. He felt (incorrectly) that he was by now inured to deprivation. For him and his own egocentric world, what counted was what 'they' thought of him. I never got to the full constitution of 'they', but he admitted that he daydreamed all the time about him and 'them', and how he fantasised conversing and smoking with them all while they drank together. He once joked that if he published his thoughts, there would be a large market for their pornographic quality. Clearly Mr J P's dreamworld kept him well thought of and warmly welcomed by his so-called private circle.

Mr J P's analysis was so different to the ordinary, everyday analytic situation, not least in the strangely restrictive world this man had lived in for over four decades. I am referring in the first instance to real interferences and inroads his illness had made upon his mind. There were his psychotic illnesses, the long alcoholic episodes and their interference with ordinary life; and the fact that he'd been enclosed for nearly two decades in a maximum security hospital. For Mr J P, the odd situation of having an analysis in a medium secure unit was curiously acceptable and easy to tolerate. The sessions themselves had a peculiarly enclosed and enclosing character, almost a claustrophilic quality, which I felt were a reflection of his mind's penumbrated quality. But behind this, he was also having the opportunity of experiencing a long-term relationship of total privacy and primacy. He was the subject of interest, though sometimes unfortunately only to myself (which in the perverse areas of his mind served their own purpose). He could be as delinquently careless, even as mad, as he wished to be and there was always a figure listening to him and caring about him – a situation Mr J P had never known.

I was perturbed by the perverse quality of Mr J P's behaviour with me, which would vary from sleepiness and inattentiveness to paroxysmal episodes of sleepiness of almost narcoleptic intensity. On the other hand there were periods of manic chatting and gossiping. These patterns were linked to his identification with his heavy drinking father and his own feeling of himself as being like his father, a man of poor status and little respect, which he was busy denying by his behaviour patterns. Later, the perverse character of his behaviour was further linked to his periods of homosexual prostitution, when he enjoyed not the physical, but what he called the social lives of these relationships; some casual, others repetitious. Gradually a more thoughtful person began to emerge; unfortunately, even this had a quality of ambiguity and cynical jokiness.

In one particular session he had decided (on his way to the session) that he would like to, or perhaps that he would, smoke. He had previously given up smoking during sessions. He felt that we were beginning to recognise his capacity to be provocatively aggressive because he knew that I disliked his smoking, and I felt he was behaving in this way to me. In the session he became silent after a while. I was suddenly doubtful about the sincerity of his presentation, as if I were being invited to believe something that I would later feel foolish about having believed. I shared my doubt with him, and added that he didn't know if he was being sensible or trying to please or trick me. He replied that he was having difficulty in keeping me out of his pornographic conversations that he had with himself. I said that he felt relieved that I'd openly questioned his sincerity, that he was afraid of corrupting me as he did his own mind, sometimes consciously, with his fairy stories, or more seriously by his behaviour, as had happened in his index offence. I said that all this occurred when this time it was he himself who had not kept his promise to himself not to smoke in the session. He then spoke about his anxieties about the future, as to where he was going to live and work when we ended his treatment. He said he looked so much like the comedian on the TV who could distort his face so completely and become so unlike himself, but at the same time become the person his face was alluding to. I felt he was talking about his weird identifications again, and their distorting effect upon his mind and behaviour, and how easily he lost his sense of self. This session was typical of the last few months of his stay on the unit, which gave us the opportunity to reflect on the kind of treatment his illness required. His serious problem in this and other sessions was that a joke could rebound; and he could be left feeling empty of future and purpose. The joke is however also serious, in that his mind is distorted into a belief that it can't work properly and he feels freakish.

In later sessions, the metaphor of the comedian with the distorting face was replaced by the various psychiatrists he'd known over the years, who had avoided knowing about his mind and its vagaries by being very friendly and talking in advisory generalisations. As he said himself, 'Fancy advising me!' These denigrating portrayals were a graphic re-presentation of his own previous thoughtless and somewhat condescending attitude to himself. This outlook lay at the centre of the problem of tricking, of being tricked, and of trickery itself. He felt that he had either tricked the doctors into stupidly believing in a potential in him which he couldn't possibly maintain, or that they now contained his own trickery and condescension. This is why he felt so relieved in the session I have described when I queried his sincerity. At the same time, life had tricked him, by giving him so many talents but not the equipment to use them. And this sad situation carried the unhappy identification with his father who drank and had no status, a fact which was relieved by further drinking.

Mr J P ended treatment and left with an awareness of his aggressive behaviour and potential, and its role in the index offence. He asked, 'Was I born insane, or did something make me insane?' I suppose the answers might be 'Yes, you had a predilection' (though I didn't know enough about his earlier years) and 'Yes' to the fact that something(s) had affected him to give rise to his insanity. He also knew that there were times when the only thing that interested him was drinking. Maybe it would have been more profitable if we had met 30 years earlier: I am not sure. However, he had become interested in himself and the sessions, not in a narcissistic fashion, which was his usual model, but introspectively and seriously – interested in the actual person he was.

What I've said about this patient, which I could equally say about any of the others in this series, is that they are victims of mixed conditions, and no matter whether we call them schizo-affective states or mixed states, their total intolerance for any depressive experience leads to a need to act out physically. Such patients can be differentiated from other mixed states by virtue of their life histories, in which loss has been psychotically denied. If they are exposed endogenously and possibly externally to such losses, they and the public become dangerously and unnecessarily exposed. These cases have another characteristic – they are almost, but not quite, importunate: they're dying to talk to somebody. Therefore they are approachable and responsive and willing to tell you what's going on inside them, though they are often not particularly aware of the significance of what they're saying. They are lost souls waiting for somebody to care for them. They seldom find this, except in the psychotic areas of their minds. This state of co-operation fluctuates, and can be replaced by rebellious resistance and absenting. In these patients mood changes, irritability, and a sense of total dissatisfaction with self, and its converse, manic happiness and dramatic storytelling, have to be noted as dangerous prodromal signs, which in turn leads to a repetitive doing of mental state examinations during the course of therapy, and particularly during ongoing care. Their minds, and their emotional contents, are barometers of significant changes which have to be noted.

The questions that have to be answered are these. Why is there a discriminatory or selective capacity for psychological projection? Why the incapacity for ridding the mind, in these men, of a particular form of depression? Concrete thinking, and projective mechanisms are very commonly found in schizophrenia and other severely disturbed individuals who can be violent: what are the specific differences in this group? The features which start to differentiate these patients when their history is studied are: (a) have they sublimated their aggressive instincts, and if there's a disturbance in the degree of sublimation, are such patients capable of full symbolisation? (b) their lives have been punctuated by profound series of losses, real or imagined. Our Mr J P overcomes loss or threatened loss of his objects by precipitately losing them or abandoning them to protect himself from the painful experience of passively experiencing loss. How do such patients experience projection? The symbol is produced of the original internal idea, which is felt now to be installed elsewhere than in their own minds. In Mr J P's case, the symbol of his mind's freedom from an unconscious awareness of its murderousness towards its object – the nice lady at the welfare – is symbolised by the appearance of suicidal ideas in the mind of the victim. In other words, the delusion is the symbol of a successful projection. I'm suggesting that there is a defective symbolisation of loss in all of these patients, and that because of unsublimated aggressive instincts and the inhibition of the activity of the instrument that initiates the symbol formation, namely projection or projective identification, symbolisation cannot take place as it ordinarily does. I have a suspicion that the absence of an original object into which they could project feelings, particularly in Mr J P's case, exaggerates this inhibition and increases the need for violent physical muscularity to replace the failed projection. If there's concretisation in these patients, it seems to me to be specifically to keep good objects in concretely, which hardly facilitates splitting of the mind and later projection.

I now want to look at three patients who suffered catastrophic losses, but dealt with them quite differently. The first was a young woman who happened to be the first psychotic case I ever saw. I was a medical student (a long, long time ago) and I was doing my practical midwifery training. It had been a beautiful Summer Bank Holiday, and I had had the day off from the midwifery hospital. I'd been out with a girl all day. We'd bathed in the sea, and as evening approached she brought me back to the hospital. I was totally unprepared for what was to happen. A young woman had been delivered of a dead baby two days before, and somehow or other nobody had told her what was going to happen during her antenatal care, and nobody had told her that the baby had died *in utero* some weeks before. As I walked into the hospital, I was informed that it was my clinical duty as a medical student to 'special' this poor patient. Nursing staff, for some strange reason, were not permitted to undertake such duties, nor to look after a psychotic patient. As I entered the room she looked at me, and said: 'I know where my husband is. I know where he is now – he's in the room in the red building behind the magistrate's court.' The magistrate's court was quite near to the hospital, and I knew exactly what she was referring to. She was referring to the police mortuary, where victims of violent death were held waiting for their post mortems. Despite my profound and repetitively stupid reassurances, young Mrs G maintained her delusional belief about her husband's fate, and she claimed she had seen his body.

I spent many hours with her. My fellow medical students were frightened of her; all of them hated anything connected with psychiatry. I found out how Mrs G knew about the red building. A cousin's mother had been killed in a street accident, and someone in a neighbouring street had been murdered in a street fight, and she had accompanied her cousin to claim the body. At no stage did she ever mention the dead baby; nor did I. It is possible to imagine, with the benefit of hindsight, the following mental scenario in Mrs G. She felt unconsciously murderous towards her husband for making a dead baby, and putting it inside her. Another possibility is that she projected her own murderous guilt about her dead baby and her role in it into her husband, which 'killed' him. Or both. It really doesn't matter which it is.

After some days Mrs G was transferred to the local mental hospital, but, shortly afterwards, I started my undergraduate psychiatric training at the local mental hospital, and on my second visit, which happened to be on the female side, I saw Mrs G in the garden of the ward. Being curious, and a friendly sort of chap, I went up to her to say 'Hello, how are you?' She replied that she had no idea who I was, nor did she know how I knew her. And she walked away. Mrs G could not have suffered a more catastrophic loss; she'd expected a healthy, live baby, and as far as I know, she never violently attacked anyone except her own mind and its memories and its contents. The narcissistic blow to me was enormous. Even nowadays I can only offer the following to account for her behaviour. She could symbolise loss in this complicated way. You could say she could tolerate delusional widowhood better than the awfulness of a loss of a child in such terrible circumstances. But what particular structure of her mind she possessed I don't know now, and I can't guess about it. And I certainly didn't know then. She certainly had enough to feel murderous about. She never complained about the hospital and of the doctors therein.

The next patient is Mr K W who came to us, like Mr J P, for rehabilitation. He had spent many years in a maximum security hospital, despite his apparent youthfulness, and he was referred to us so that he could be rehabilitated. I looked up the word 'rehabilitation' in the OED: 'To restore by formal act or declaration a person degraded or attainted to former privileges, rank and possessions. To re-establish a person's good name or memory by authoritative pronouncement. To re-establish the character or reputation of a person or thing.' Finally: 'To restore to a previous condition; to set up again in proper condition.' All this for poor Mr K W, who, despite many years in a maximum security hospital, firmly believed that he came from a place from within the Bermuda Triangle. His country of origin had a peculiar name, but there was nothing peculiar about the people of his country. They thought only of higher things. They were cultured and peaceful, and light years ahead of ordinary earthlings in their thoughts and practices. And he and his team had been sent to help out where they thought it was necessary on earth. He heard that Mrs W's son had been killed in a motorcycle accident, and feeling very sorry for Mrs W suffering such a dreadful loss, he had projected himself into the body of Mrs W's son and taken over his history and his memory. He knew everything there was to know about him; unfortunately the delusional story therefore was that he had a delusion that he was himself. And therefore, in becoming Mrs W's son, he'd enabled himself to have this strange experience. Mr K W had had a catastrophic life. From the very beginning he was abandoned by Mrs W, a West Indian lady, and taken into care, but unfortunately periodically returned to her. He grew up mostly in various institutions and boarding establishments. He was attracted to white, middle-class boys, one of whom many years before he'd held hostage. Mr K W always stoutly denied any aggressive violence, and on one occasion there was a suggestion of – but never proved – sexual interference.

Mr K W could be said to have never had anything much to lose. His good objects were delusional, seductive, constantly available and interchangeable. He was a pleasant, friendly, talkative young man; street-wise and deceptively intelligent sounding. His omnipotent capacity to replace any threatened awareness of change in his mental life was brilliant. He hallucinated contact with the other members of his group frequently; they were all seriously concerned with helping the people on earth, he believed. He denied the significance of his reality position; he awaited the arrival of materials to build his spaceship, which would take him back to his own country. Such an undertaking would mean that some other figure from his country would have to undertake to do a locum. The central point about Mr K W is that his delusional psychosis insulated his mind against any awareness of loss. To what extent should we interfere with his mental state? When he is in the community all goes desperately wrong. His capacity to believe in his brilliant inner world also sometimes goes wrong: he then wants to be a fortunate white boy who has everything that he feels now he never had. To what further possessions and positions could we rehabilitate poor Mr K W? Of this wonderful mental prestidigitation of replacing anything with something else? His interest to us lies in how he deals with psychic loss, but this doesn't diminish the enormity of his problems and his awful future. I shall return to Mr K W.

Mr V L, a professional man, is the third patient I wish to discuss. He was sent for treatment under the most unusual circumstances a very long time ago; I think he's now long dead. He was advised by the senior partners of his firm to seek treatment, because his behaviour at work was felt to be intolerable. He quarrelled with everybody, took no advice and argued arrogantly, and not very cleverly, at conferences at his work. Those junior to him found his sneering, aggressive condescension intolerable. His relationship to clients was becoming costly because he was equally overbearing towards them. His wife was in the psychiatric profession, and she had been warned that he might be sacked. She herself was related to the senior partner. The original referral for treatment turned out disastrously. He stalked his female psychoanalyst. He followed her into her country home and the police had to be called. She refused to see him any more, and felt deeply shaken by the whole miserable experience. I was invited to take over and help in what was a very difficult situation. I regretted agreeing to help every single day. He treated me with the same disdain and condescension that he treated the junior people in his office. Anything I offered about him was waved away as being juvenile at best, and silly at worst. He would sleep though a large part of his sessions with me, claiming that these naps restored him to a state of peaceful, sensible equilibrium. His only trouble was having to wake up to hear me offer some rubbishy explanation.

Gradually a little truth filtered through into the sessions. His parents, he felt, were part of a *folie à deux*. They were both deluded. They believed that he was their son, which was quite impossible, because they were both silly Jewish peasants, and therefore how could he be their child? Their delusional state did not prevent him from relying on his father to sponsor his membership of his big firm, nor did it prevent him from taking money from his father for a variety of other reasons. Mr V L was a gambler, and therefore obviously regularly short of money. Of course, he spoke of this 'minor trouble' as if it were a sort of upper-class joke. Most importantly, he was stricken by attacks of enormous hypochondriacal anxiety, reaching, on occasion, an almost nihilistic delusional intensity in which he felt he contained no vital internal organs. He had driven two physicians quite mad with demands for investigations, and they had both refused to see him any more, finding his hypochondriacal certitudes too much to bear. From our point of view, this latter symptom is fascinating, as it was the only truthful thing about this man and about the way he lived his life. He had created an entire nothingness of his internal world, and his periods of paranoid delusions were unfortunately for him the practical psychic truth. So the hypochondriacal attacks, which told of his mind's propagandistic assaults on his own awareness of who and what he was, were the only truthful thing about him. Everybody contained, for him, a destructive attack on his fantasy world, by knowing or possibly knowing who he was.

All this appeared in bits and pieces during some of his sessions. Some he told, some I inferred – or 'interfered', according to him. I would have called them at best interpretations or at least attempts at interpretations. One day he announced that he was very well, and was sure that he would remain so. He had hidden from me that whilst seeing me for treatment he had been receiving tuition from a Catholic priest, and he had now converted and felt quite wonderful. He was leaving his wife – he had met and wooed a beautiful woman – so thank you very much. This man and Mr K W possessed similar mental equipment. I was searching for a word for the capacity that these two men possess – I was talking to a colleague, Robin Anderson, and describing to him this capacity to change their internal objects at will, that was more than denial, even of a psychotic intensity – and he called my attention to the capacity of certain computers to change the faces of objects, and the fact that this process was called morphing. And from that we then developed the word metamorphosing.

Mr K W and Mr V L metamorphosed their objects at will, almost as supernatural, quasi-religious phenomena. Why Mr K W was so pleasant about it and Mr V L so amazingly unlikeable I don't know. But neither ever lost their objects. They simply changed them into the Bermuda Triangle variety or to Catholic icons. Loss never occurs, and despite desperate provocation, they never have to project violently. They concretise mental losses into anybody around them.

I can now go back to poor Mr M B with his problem of the black and white dog crossing the road and informing upon him, as if he were really the culprit. His victim was now the culprit, and his victim contained everything that was troubling or dogging the mind of Mr M B. The little fair-haired boy in the ward would similarly have been converted into being a troubled boy. Mr M B found each day evidence of what he lost, either black or white young men, and in his mind they were what he felt to be pure and untroubled. Mr M B had to rid his mind of his conflict, but it has to be remembered that Mr M B had a schizophrenic conflict, not any ordinary, everyday, should-I-shouldn't-I nonsense. For Mr M B part of the conflict was characterised by either mutual cruelty or destruction. For him, things coming together meant that they attacked one another. Pictures in his mind of his parents coming together produced this same vicious duality.

I wished we had had the facilities to treat him. What I don't know is: why didn't he, following such an awesome schizophrenic conflict, have the delusion that he was either white or black? I've thought about this, and I think he was so identified with parts of his parents psychically, and their lives so conflictually played out, both in reality and in Mr M B's envious, jealous mind, that he was trapped in this schizophrenic impasse. So, ironically, all of this is expressed by the sad remark: 'If the bloody black and white dog hadn't crossed the road, nothing would have happened.' If his black and white parents hadn't crossed into his mind so often and so destructively, Mr M B might have been spared. He never was.

References

SOHN, L (1995) 'Unprovoked assaults – making sense of apparently random violence', *International Journal of Psycho-Analysis, 76*, pp.565–75

2

Michael Conran

Sorrow, vulnerability and madness

You think I'll weep;
No, I'll not weep:
I have full cause of weeping, but this heart
Shall break into a hundred thousand flaws
Or ere I'll weep. O Fool! I shall go mad.
William Shakespeare, King Lear Act II Scene iv

The paper I am about to read is one I have given before and it presents me with a dilemma which I shall now explain. It is in fact part of a chapter of a doctoral thesis written more than a quarter of a century ago; and it is my intention to read it in its original, that is to say, unrevised form. To be sure, I could not, or should not, have written it in this form now. Which is to say it is scarcely to be judged now as a case history, even less as a scientific paper. I now like to think of it as a story, though if anyone had suggested that to me when I wrote it I should have bristled with indignation. This was written before I trained as a psychoanalyst and I did not then appreciate the everlasting importance and strength of the story. Modern medicine came to abjure the story generally under the contemptuous and dismissive epithet, 'anecdotal evidence', which, however statistically justified, diverts attention away from the central importance to everyone of us, as to every patient, of his own story. Much of the business of psychoanalysis is to help the patient to find a story in the first place, and then one with which he can live. Pirandello's most celebrated play, *Six characters in search of an author*, does, in some sense, illustrate this; but the quotation I most cherish is that of Isaac Bashevis Singer who said, 'The story is everything. If the Iliad had come to us a commentary by Marx or as an interpretation by Freud, nobody would read it.' In another context he said, 'A story must be a love story. Many writers have attempted to write a story which is not a love story and they have always failed.'

Each time I give this paper I discover something new in it of which I was unaware, or at least unconscious, when I wrote it. Which is, to my mind, an added tribute to the importance of the story. For example it reports such things as 'he had never wept in his life'. At the time I believed this to be true, inasmuch as it never crossed my mind to question the truth of what I had been told. It seems to me to be of utmost importance we respect our gullibility, which is a mark of our vulnerability and hunger to understand and learn. (Ernest Jones once remarked upon Freud's gullibility.) If one does not let in, admit, what one is told, how else can one come to reflect upon it, to value it, and only then, perhaps, to question it? My dilemma focuses upon one part of me which wishes simply to tell you the story and then sit down; whereas another part, less courageous – or less arrogant – feels a need to offer a more scientific justification in the traditional form of intro-duction, discussion and conclusions. The less courageous part of me is going to prevail and I shall proceed therefore with both slices of bread before offering you the meat in the sandwich that is the story.

In the 1960s, there existed at Shenley Hospital, a large state mental hospital 17 miles north-west of London, an unusual psycho-analytic ambience. The hospital was, and had been since the war, a Mecca for psychoanalytic trainees. This was due, in the main, to one psychiatric consultant, Dr S T Hayward, himself a psychoanalyst, but an unusual one inasmuch as he fostered and provoked psychoanalytic thinking within the setting of the most seriously mentally ill. A man who had an unusual capacity for the containment of projections, by which I mean the acting out of staff, especially medical staff, at all levels, he insistently promoted, by encouragement and support, the pursuit of a psychoanalytic psychiatry. The promotion was not formu-lated in any categorical way: it was more by example and enablement. An implicit valuation was put upon free association in discussion, abjuring that omniscient quest for exactness which is the mark of those in the pursuit of some final truth. I do not know of anyone who so explicitly suggested and taught that the patient had a right to his illness. Elsewhere (Conran 1984) I have dwelt upon this as it concerns the mentally, in contrast to the physically, ill. The setting then is one which hardly exists today within the NHS, and we can, if we wish, discuss this. In those days the hospital was still segregated sexually, and the division, one of three, which Hayward led was the male divi-sion, the other two being female. Hayward held to a view that the young schizophrenic, especially in his first breakdown (so-called), was still susceptible to being helped significantly to change and therefore something special and separate was warranted. An unit, a 20-bed villa called 'Villa 21', was therefore set aside, wherein a young male schizo-phrenic could find an opportunity – not always a very welcome one – to enter into relationships with nurses and a doctor seeking to under-stand rather than cure him. Time does not permit me to dwell upon the life and work of 'Villa 21', which had a psychoanalytic conception, followed by an infantile period wherein it achieved a certain fame or notoriety through Cooper (Cooper 1967). I was the psychiatric registrar in analysis following Cooper. I worked in 'Villa 21' for eight years. I obtained my MD for an explicitly psychoanalytic thesis in respect of 'Schizophrenia'. It was the most privileged time of my working life.

I turn now to what would ordinarily be regarded as the discussion in an orthodox presentation. The patients' first admission to hospital is only one way we, society, respond to anxiety which can no longer be contained within the home, *ie* the family. Moreover, it is, in my judgement, better to be understood as a 'break-out', than a 'breakdown'. Defences – intrapsychic and interpersonal – fail and come to be seen for what they are, maladaptive, and ultimately useless in the struggle for a separate existence. The transferences made are immediate and overwhelming such that society's agents, fearful of the arousal of their own individual unresolved conflicts about separateness, seek to control and shut up that which is feared as seeking to break out. Such is our fear of unknown feelings and thoughts finding expression in words that the schizophrenic is shut up physically and then verbally shut up with drugs in the pursuit of what is called 'treatment'. I am therefore advancing a contention that the first breakdown (*sic*) of a young schizophrenic is a positive act of self-assertion, it is – however bizarre – the exhibition of such ego as there is. It is, however disguised, a plea for help and, in a most peculiar way, a statement of health or, as I prefer to call it – wellness. He is well-enough to be able, that is to assert his right, to be ill-enough to get to hospital, or whatever. His quest for what Sullivan called 'security operations' (Sullivan 1953) distinguishes him from those too ill to get help. Those people die. They are so undeserving they have no right to be ill, in the sense of being ill in relation to others.

It will be evident that classical psychoanalysis, of whatever school or group, is not pertinent in this extreme setting, one wherein relationships with doctors and nurses are immediate and concrete. This does not, as is now generally well recognised, mitigate against the formation of transferences which are immediate, intense and usually primitive, such as to evoke countertransferences of a corresponding nature. They are, in my experience, intense, specific and often very disagreeable. Love, hate and all manner of passionate savagery will be available, evoking a psychotic counter-transference. A worker in this field is soon made aware of why it is a psychotherapeutic approach to the schizophrenic is shunned; and of a need for something more than supervision, which might be better called protective husbandry. Yet there is, in my view, no other way to make sense of the relationships in which the schizophrenic engages than by analysis of the transference, and that its value to the patient lies, in the first instance, not through interpretation made to him, but by interpretation to doctor and nurse so as to enable constructive relationships to continue. In any event, interpretation to the patient of apparently unconscious feeling and phantasy is likely only to tell him that of which he is already only too conscious.

It hardly needs saying that the age and circumstances of the schizophrenic's first admission present the staff with a family in distress. An empathic relationship with the family is one which the doctor may or may not choose to delegate to others, *eg* social workers. This is not my choice. Much is to be learnt from interaction with the family, one wherein the doctor is truthful, says what he knows and what he does not know, is sensitive to the family's difficulties and seeks to reduce, rather than to emphasise, guilt. A relationship with mother will invariably expose a transference every bit as specific as her son's, such that the doctor gains a very specific feeling of what it is like to be her schizophrenic son – even to be mistaken for him in her confusion – except, of course, the doctor can escape, recognising the symbolic significance of his encounters (Conran 1976). Thus it becomes apparent that the schizophrenic, as any adolescent, is confronted with a confusion about an internal object and a real external one. In the midst of an essentially paranoid relationship to both internal and external objects, he struggles to repair or to reconstruct (Rey 1988) an internal object, one such as to give him a good enough mother (Winnicott 1965), from whom he can then safely separate. His dilemma is that he needs to, but cannot, separate himself from the damaged persecuting mother in what is often referred to as the symbiotic relationship, one for which, in my view, a syncitial relationship would be a better choice of biological metaphor. The psychoanalytic principle of following the patient is expectant, unintrusive and reminiscent of the naturalist. It is, in my submission, unarguably scientific. Now I want to tell you the story and to remind you of D H Lawrence's caveat 'Never trust the artist. Trust the tale.'

At half-past three of a February morning the police were called to a hospital to help the staff deal with an 'unknown man', who did not know who he was, waved his arms, grimaced and refused to speak. He was despatched to a mental hospital outside London where he arrived at 5 o'clock. He was said to be 'quiet and co-operative' but told a nurse he could not remember his name or address. Later that morning he recalled he was Thomas Leary, that he was 17 years old, and his address where he lived with his parents. Within two days he came to us in Villa 21.

Tom was 5'8" tall and weighed 126 lb, though he seemed to be slightly built. His aspect was compelling. He wore his black hair long, with long sideboards and a black, mandarin-type moustache fashionable in his age-group. He wore large, black-rimmed spectacles corrected for astigmatism, which gave an impression of magnifying his eyes. Because of his small face, his hair, sideboards, moustache and glasses seemed to dominate his features. His mouth, though full, was restricted as to free range of expression. When closed, his lips conveyed defiance; when parted, his teeth were closed and he appeared to speak or grimace through them. The overall impression was of someone who ought to be frightening, yet who, like a child, did not quite manage to be so; of one who conveyed a feeling of being more frightened than frightening, as he hid, so to speak, behind a barricade of hair, glasses and teeth. Though he might conceive of himself in demoniacal terms, he was received as a tragic and comical figure. He wore jeans and very large shoes which at first glance looked like boots many sizes too big for him. He could have been a character created by Walt Disney.

My earliest interviews with him were spent mostly in silence. After one of them, he sprang up, drank several cups of water from the tap and said to the nurse, 'Has the witch doctor gone?' (the habit of drinking large volumes of water in times of emotional upheaval was to have significance). With a nurse of his own age, he could be more talkative. He thought his brain cells were dying, saying, 'What's the use of talking, nothing can replace brain cells.' He said his father did not accept the fact that he was ill. He worried about his job: 'I must keep working to keep sane.' His parents visited him one evening and father told the nurse that the only thing wrong with Thomas was that he liked having his own way. For the past few months he had been staying out later and later, and would not tell father where he had been. Father told him 'either you come in at a decent hour or not at all.' He continued coming in at 1·30 – 2·00 am. Father finally locked the door and he was forced to knock them up.

Tom was very quiet and solitary, seeking to please by helping in the villa. He told the nurse he 'must work to stop from thinking'. Gradually, as he relaxed and worked less, he was able to complain that his brain was 'stuffed up' and that he was 'depressed'. After he had been with us a month, he was able to tell me a little of his feeling that he was not sure if he had thoughts. His body and his mind were separated and he indicated this by marking a line above his mouth. This was followed by an ironical laugh. He thought his difficulties began when he was 13 or 14 but could not remember. Some days later I thought he might be able to tell me more. He began suspiciously, saying there was nothing to tell. He chain-smoked and said, 'These are my time sticks.' 'Only got to wait for two revolutions, and it would all be gone, all the faces.' Since I could make little of this, I asked him to tell me about his parents. His father was 'very, very tolerant'. 'He's half dead isn't he?' I asked him what his father did. Tom did not feel he ought to tell me – 'mustn't let people break into my square like that'. How old was mother and what did she do? 'I don't know. How would I know? I wouldn't know, would I?' He was angry with me, and then laughed ironically – to himself.

Wherever I pried, he shut me out.

He thought he was born two years after mother had given birth to stillborn twins. 'So you are the oldest child?' 'My Dad's the oldest, isn't he?' It was true about the stillborn twins. There was also a younger brother of 16 and a sister of 11. In due course he told me he had been 'a gypsy' for three or four months, living out on the road. He thought of himself as several people. For example, one who went to work. He liked his younger sister, but hated his brother. What did his brother do? 'He's an electronics engineer, isn't he?' 'I'm positive and he's negative; they're repelling aren't they?' Then, as an afterthought, 'or I'm nega- tive and he's negative, or I'm positive and he's positive'. 'I thought for a long time he was negative and I was positive and drawn to him.' 'So you don't hate him all the time?' 'No.'

He said he did not feel anything about his mother, and was puzzled. He did not know why that was. 'She's so different; all chopped up into little pieces all the time.' She was quite different, he said, when she saw him in hospital, from at home. His father worried him. He dreamt someone broke into the house and tried to kill him. He saw his father's face. But there was another face in the house (in the dream). The killer seemed to be stronger than his real father. The killer father went under the bed. The real father would not believe him and told him to go back to sleep. He returned to bed and the killer re-emerged. The beds in the villa reminded him of this dream.

He went on to speak of 'the face of my father, with something flaring, fiery and wild inside him'. 'Really he's calm to the point of unbelief – suddenly he's wild – it's the constant nagging from Mum – from early morning to late at night – it makes him wild.' He told me he felt he had never met his parents properly. 'I nearly met them once, when we went on holiday together. But he done something and has gone foreign again.' (A long time later, very shortly before she died, I heard about this holiday from Mrs Leary. For a few days she had felt the family might enjoy their holiday together, but Mr Leary found an excuse to return to London to work.)

'I think sometimes I'm in somebody else's mind.' He was sure he had two brothers, besides his younger one. They revolved round him. One was 'self-conscious and apathetic'. 'The other one, the one who's gone, found some joy.'

'I feel outside everything. I can't get involved in anything can I?' Of his plans for the future – 'a load of time; revolutions of the clock; time eats into me – sometimes I'd like to smash that clock'. 'I feel my parents tear me up into bits.' Tom was an Irish cockney and when he came to us he took his religion seriously. He kept his rosary and a missal by his bed.

His parents came to see me on St Patrick's Day. Both were from Ireland. Mother was a small, restless woman with a sallow drawn face, in her mid-forties. She looked younger but the dominating aspect of her personality was her restless grimacing. She looked nauseated and made a repeated grimace as if something putrid was being pushed in front of her. Father was quiet and softly spoken. When he spoke, he stood up, to attention, as if he were a good boy reporting – a witness to some misdeed – to his headmaster. He was a self-employed painter and decorator; and he worked extremely hard.

The silence was broken by mother declaring that if only Thomas would 'get his hair cut and his whiskers shaved off and look human'.

I invited her to expand on this and she spoke contemptuously in a rejecting way about him. Father's accent, though soft, had a whining quality. He was more mildly disapproving. The contrast in parental attitudes could be summarised as mother's rejection and father's reproof. Father took over the conversation, being better able to talk coherently. Mother grimaced, laughed and made peculiar gestures. She could not, it seemed to me, converse rationally at all, but confined herself to complaints and criticisms. Father told me how, on the night of Tom's admission, they had locked him out, fed up as they were with his obstinate behaviour. They did not seem to know where Tom went at night. (I was to learn subsequently that he used to seek refuge in public houses. He told me he came to regard the public house as home – where he could keep warm and was not constantly nagged.) I wondered if they had not thought of seeking help with Tom, sooner than lock him out all night. They seemed to think this preposterous, so I enquired of friends whose assistance they might enlist. Mother replied they never went to relatives for help. Mother then complained of Tom not 'communicating', as she put it. I found it very difficult to say anything myself to her which I thought she was able to listen to. I invited her to tell me about the twins she had lost as a means of establishing a dialogue in respect of something she might care to talk about. She spoke little about this, so I enquired about Tom's birth. She seemed to remember this as a good time. There had only been one happier time in her life, when she was single, working with other girls in a munitions factory. It seemed to me she had enjoyed Tom's infancy and I asked her if this was so. She had breast-fed him for five months, but saying this made her embarrassed, though I thought she rather enjoyed her discomfiture. She said it was getting hot and started to take off some clothes. I said it was all very distressing and she said she was afraid of going mad if she let her distress show, and would 'end up in this place'. Conversation with her was difficult as she spoke often in opposites: *ie* saying the opposite of what she meant. This made me confused and my difficulty in sorting out what she really meant caused father some wry amusement, as he winked knowingly at the psychiatric social worker who was with us.

Tom remained very paranoid in respect of myself and the nurses for some weeks. But I saw quite a lot of him when there was a group of patients. He was bright, witty and could make a slightly bizarre remark which would cause everyone to laugh. In due course I was to understand that having made me laugh, he could look directly at me and examine me. I was then (laughing) no longer 'watching' him. Some time later he became very depressed but would not talk about it. He became withdrawn and spoke about leaving hospital. He was unworthy and did not care what became of him. (He did not disclose what I subsequently learned, that his mother was ill and that his father had been goading him into leaving.)

The Villa outing to the seaside took place in June and we went in a charabanc to Walton. It was a fine, warm day and I dozed off to sleep in the coach. Tom had declared his intention to have a few beers and I did not see him until we returned to the coach. I had bought a plastic windmill to take home for my daughter, which I carried. We stood eating sandwiches before getting into the coach to return to Shenley and I asked Tom what sort of day he had had. He replied, pointing at the windmill, 'I never expected to see you with something like that.' I said, 'You mean only lunatics and children carry things like this?' He laughed and said, 'Yes! that's right.' I said, 'Well, perhaps there's a time and place to be mad and childish.' Then he confided in me, 'Actually, what got me was seeing you asleep in the coach. I didn't know you could do that.' My first association to this remark was of urinating, but it seemed such a bizarre association, I said, 'You mean it makes me rather like you: if I can sleep like you then my body works like yours in other ways.' 'That's right,' he said, 'still, I didn't think you would go to sleep.' He got on the coach and came and sat beside me all the way home. In the course of conversation he told me about all his awful feelings of being 'stuffed full of shit all the time'. I was struck by the sudden willingness to allow a spontaneous exchange, other than as an entertainer. I realised that being asleep had been important in another sense. He had been able to scrutinise me at leisure for the first time. I had relaxed control in his presence. I had dared to become overtly vulnerable, off-guard, in the presence of someone as poisonous and dangerous as he felt himself to be. Tom never wore his spectacles after this episode.

He continued to develop and exploit his capacity to make himself an object of staff affection, and to become more spontaneous in ventilating his disagreeable feelings. However he would have nothing to do with women. Then he suddenly disappeared and we found out that he had gone home. I telephoned him but he would not speak to me. We learnt that his mother was very seriously ill. We telephoned now to enquire about her. He spoke to a nurse and said that his mother was dying. If she died he would commit suicide. It became necessary to telephone daily to show Tom we were still very much alive – alive in the sense of being interested in him. There was, so to speak, another kind of mother who was not going to die, who cared about him and who was not going to cast him adrift. We telephoned daily for two weeks and he then returned to the Villa.

Tom was very depressed. He was unworthy of being in Villa 21. He felt himself to be full of diseases and ought to be discharged as he would infect the other patients. His mother had been taken to the Renal Dialysis Unit at St Paul's Hospital in an effort to save her life, but he thought she was going to die. He was morose, surly and withdrawn.

During the next two weeks I noticed that neither the nurses nor I now were much concerned about this predicament. Here was a young lad whose mother was dying and yet there was an apparent response of indifference. I called him into the office and asked him how he felt about his mother's illness. He shrugged and made some grimaces. We sat together for some while and I said, 'You cannot weep'. He grimaced more. I began to sense a feeling towards weeping stirring in me and said 'I think you need me to weep for you.' I then learnt he had never wept in his life.

I asked Tom if he would like to go and see his mother. He would not say. I suggested we might go together (I had not at this time formulated my method of working coincidentally with mothers, and was therefore following a feeling that for no specific reason seemed to me important: namely, that Tom's inability to have feelings of grief was somehow connected with my visiting mother). I telephoned the doctor in charge of Mrs Leary, who disclosed his anxiety for her survival; and said he would welcome my visit. I arranged to go on a Thursday evening; and as Tom could not make up his mind whether or not he would accompany me, I would come to the hospital at 6·00 pm and proceed from there with or without him.

The events that ensued were remarkable. However, I want to call to attention the bizarre association I had on the summer outing in respect of urinating – before I knew anything about Mrs Leary's chronic nephritis or Tom's incapability of weeping.

After a very long day's work, which included much motoring in and out of London, I called in at my home before proceeding to Shenley and then the further journey into London and back with Tom. The point I am seeking to make is that, on this evening, I was sufficiently tired to be more than usually vulnerable. At home I drank three cups of tea before setting off. This was the first event which was most unusual. I had learnt that if I drank one cup of tea before motoring to London, on arrival I should have to urinate. More than one cup of tea was to court discomfiture. Three cups was, in common parlance, mad!

On my arrival at Villa 21, I found Tom standing at the sink drinking successive cups of water. The whole afternoon had been spent in preparation for our visit and he had made himself as smart as he could. There was a lot of final fuss about a raincoat and then we set off. I drove through Hendon (where Tom lived) while he talked continuously and happily about the locality. I was disarmed during this part of the journey by his demonstration of his limited knowledge of Yiddish, and by his insight into the ways of Jewish Londoners. During the next part of the journey he poured out an account of his symptoms – how he felt 'full of shit' and how he could 'never have a good shit'; how he could not tolerate work with the continual feeling he was being watched. There was much elaboration of this.

I had not been to St Paul's Hospital before and had some difficulty in locating it in the dark. Moreover the street system of St Giles Circus was unfamiliar and I made two circuits before arriving in front of the hospital. I was by now extremely weary. During the last part of the journey Tom had expressed anxiety about urinating. He needed to and would there be a possibility of doing so at the hospital? Nothing I said reassured him that this was certain; and this conversation continued while I tried to locate the hospital. Finally, as I parked the car, he turned to me and said, 'I hope you are not going to attack my mother.' I was startled by this and said, 'What do you mean?' 'Well', he said, 'last time you met her you attacked her.' 'How?' I asked, now feeling guilty. 'You asked her questions about the breast,' he said, embarrassed to mention the word 'breast'. 'Did I?'

I got out of the car, tired, guilty and now anxious too. It had just occurred to me I did not know what I was going to say, nor indeed what I had come to the hospital to do.

We entered the hospital and searched for a lavatory for Tom. I found a series of cubicles into which Tom dashed only to find specimen bottles and funnels inside. Eventually I pointed to a large cubicle. He pushed open the door and dashed in. I waited for him but did not urinate myself.

We walked into the Dialysis Unit, I introduced myself, and the ward sister took us to Mrs Leary's bed. Mr Leary sat reading a newspaper. Tom and I stood at the foot of the bed. Father stood up and all three men stood looking at each other. It was some moments before Mrs Leary, who lay groaning and writhing in the bed, was aware of visitors. Then with very great effort she looked at me and said, 'Oh hello! Dr Conran.' She recognised me though she had met me once only, eight months previously. She looked at Tom and said, 'Who's that?'. I found myself confused by this. Then, as if the men were useless and helpless, she tried to organise us to fetch chairs and sit down. I sat beside her, Tom at the bottom of the bed.

Mrs Leary lay under a single sheet. She was yellow and thin. Her mouth was dry and her lips cracked. She moaned and sighed and appeared very tired. She was, I learnt, due for a further attempt at dialysis in the morning. Her arms and hands bore evidence of many intravenous insertions. Her restless agitation struck me forcibly that she could not tolerate the discomfort of her body and that she wished to be left in peace to die. She made an effort to apologise to me for being unable to talk to me properly.

For a few minutes I sat there feeling it would be an unwarranted interference to say anything, and with a sense of grief mounting within me. Then she turned and gasped to me, 'How is Sally?' (She must have learnt from Tom that I had a daughter by this name.) This quite overwhelmed me, and I averted my head in an effort to conceal my now irrepressible need to weep.

I recovered myself and spoke softly to her. I told her that Tom was dearly loved by the Villa staff. She said she knew – or something to that effect. I said that if we could love him she must have given him a lot of her love. She said she had, adding, 'I loved him more than the others, but I grew so afraid of him.' I said I thought I needed her to get well, and that his welfare and hers seemed to be linked in some way. She writhed and muttered something to the effect that she found herself feeling terrible, and made some complaint to me about the restriction put upon her in what she could drink. Then she tried to thank me for all I was doing for Tom, and how much it meant to her.

I asked Tom if he wished to stay with his parents for a while but he did not, saying he needed to urinate. We returned to the lavatory where again he urinated and I did not.

In the car he told me he had seen me weeping. He told me men did not weep.

I remarked that Winston Churchill had often wept in public. But he held to his belief that a man did not weep. What about his father? He said he had seen him weep, but seemed to think he was not a real man.

Two weeks later we returned and I met the doctors caring for Mrs Leary. They were puzzled. They told me she had been selected as having a good biochemical prognosis, and there had been no reason for her 'failure to respond'. There was equally no biochemical explanation for her sudden 'response' following our visit. Tom and I went to see her and she was strikingly different. I asked her if she ever wept. She thought she must have, 'long, long ago', but she could not be sure. I left Tom with her and when I returned she was sitting up nagging him insistently about something. Tom remarked she was much better.

On our third visit she was on the machine, which made a deep impression on Tom. He had no idea so much trouble would be taken for his mother. He added that he had been rather frightened by the thought that by simply breaking or cutting one of the plastic tubes, his mother could be killed.

Still he did not weep.

The episode had been a striking lesson to me of the force of projective identification. By being a mentally 'well' person, and especially in a relative state of fatigue, I was, in contrast to the schizophrenic, organised towards vulnerability (Winnicott 1968). Instead of urinating I was capable of having depressed feelings – feelings of guilt and grief – and of weeping. This need in Tom was, therefore, successfully projected into me. The 'attack' on his mother in respect of breastfeeding, with which Tom chose to make me guilty, was a projection of his own guilt in respect of his attacks on his mother's breast at a much earlier time. Confirmation of this came five months later.

Tom went to work in a nearby factory. On Saturday there was no work. The nurse said this seemed to disturb him. He was restless and sullen all the afternoon, pacing about the Villa in a raincoat and scarf. He looked thunderously angry but would not or could not talk about it. The nurse laid the dining room table for tea. Immediately everything was laid out, including teapot, milk, sugar and food, Tom came in with a stick and swept the lot to the floor. The nurse was furious. 'I took the stick away from him, opened the front door, threw him out and told him to take a walk and come back when he felt better and could talk about what was troubling him.' We must note that the attack is not made on my 'breast', but on the nurse's 'breast'. We must also note that the nurse, like his parents, threw him out; but unlike his parents the nurse told him to come back.

Five minutes later he broke a window in the Villa with a scaffold pole obtained from the neighbouring Villa. 'He was very disturbed and threatened to smash anyone who came near him,' the nurse said. The nurse continued, 'I felt ashamed of having thrown him out so I went out and brought him back to the Villa. I took him up to his bedroom and suggested he might feel better if he put on his pyjamas. He took off his raincoat, scarf and jacket, and suddenly began to cry. I sat on the edge of the bed with my arm round his shoulders for about ten minutes. He sobbed uncontrollably – I thought it would never stop – the tears streamed from his eyes. Gradually the sobbing subsided, he said he felt much better, though he still looked very woebegone. We had a cup of tea together; then I tucked him in bed and he slept for a couple of hours.'

'I felt ashamed: so I went out and brought him back.' Unlike Tom's parents he was unafraid of Tom. He was also unafraid to show Tom his own facial expression of remorse.

This case has developed further in ways just as illuminating in other respects, but this is as far as I propose to take it. The change in Tom compared with the comic and pitiable figure who came to us is remarkable to us, and more so to those who see him occasionally. Very briefly, three years in Villa 21 has witnessed Tom change into a man, though he remains a very handicapped man. When he came to us he believed the food was poisoned. Now he may, as part of a belligerent and surly outburst, declare I am probably poisoning him. One difference is that he is now able to laugh at his persecutory feeling. He is able to work from the hospital, though it remains to be seen whether he will be able to endure any work situation for an indefinite period. The most important accomplishment however lies in the fact that he no longer needs to secure relationships as an occasional comic. He has durable relationships with men; and can tolerate ordinary social contact with women, and derive satisfaction from this.

* * * * * *

The break in the story indicates where the lecture ends without further comment, leaving the audience free to question, to criticise and so take further discussion where it will. This option is not open to the reader. I shall therefore make a number of observations which, in the interests of brevity, may sometimes have a certain dogmatic flavour. And that leads straightaway into the first observation.

1   Such are the feelings of impotence and uncertainty in work with psychotic patients, alerting us, as they will, to the psychotic parts of

our own personalities, that the temptation to retreat omnisciently into dogma is as inevitable as it is irresistible. The psychoanalytic function is then to analyse the despair split off and projected into nursing staff who already have varying capacities to contain their own despair and so, in turn, will project it back into the patient or someone else in authority who is perceived capable of containing it. I do not know how the latter course is possible but for some psychoanalytic capacity in that person or persons.

2   Following from this, we recognise that the temptations of dogmatic thought lead to quite insistent claims to possess the truth. Psychiatrists most obviously are prone to make professional claims to know. However, I would say they are not alone. There are others, and I do not exclude some psychoanalysts. The exclusive possession of 'the truth' is, it seems to me, to be psychotically possessed by it.

3   Psychoanalysis has identified psychotic processes in all of us. It is all a question of degree. That being so, the individual is unique and that holds for the patient as well as for ourselves. If there is no demonstrable disease 'Schizophrenia', there are people we call schizophrenic. They also are uniquely different from each other and the rest of us. It is all a question of more and less.

4   It will be evident that my approach to my work in Villa 21 was, from the outset, empirical. I was nevertheless influenced by work known to me at that time, which was at the beginning of my career in psychiatry. It was also at the beginning of my 'career' as a patient in analysis. In eight years I would say I progressed through various levels of incompetence, always trusting my feelings and protecting my sense of humour. I also depended upon the unquestioned reliability and protection of the consultant ultimately responsible. I would say there is less need for critical supervision than for enabling husbandry, while a worker in this field develops and discovers him or herself. Frances Tustin, working with autistic children, has alluded, in some way, to this need. I will now explain some of the reading and observations which influenced me.

5   I came increasingly to recognise that the hospital was a nursing institution. This I hold to be true of any hospital, not only mental hospitals. No matter what expertise a hospital offers, without nursing, nobody will come (Conran 1991). This is a more complex matter than we realise. The work of Menzies (1960) in addressing the nursing service of a general hospital, a social system as a defence against anxiety, is seminal to any examination of nursing. However, it does not deal with mental nursing explicitly, and the transference/counter-transference phenomena inherent to the mental hospital setting. I suggest the closure of hospitals, and public disaffection with all hospitals, has less to do with money than that it reflects an unconscious perception that, since 1935, or thereabouts, technological advances, beginning with the

sulphonamides, have gradually undermined the central importance of nursing care as an expression of maternal feeling.

6   Central to the admission of the schizophrenic, as of any patient, is the unspoken communication of a need for maternal feeling expressed through nursing care. This is not a symbolic matter. It is required concretely and bodily. Words will come sooner, later or not at all. Such is the split and projection of the adult, governing part of the patient into the nurse, that psychoanalytic interpretation of the transference is most productively offered to the nurse, who now carries the unregressed, age-appropriate part of the patient. Transferences are made by patients immediately and 'all over the place', *ie* into different staff, which means the split transference needs to be identified. This was not evident to me at once. When it was, its identification and interpretation was, from the outset, haphazard. This is realistic and needs no apology. This work is not done by 'experts' (for which we may sometimes be thankful). It is a human endeavour and so needs to be regarded humanely.

7   The ability of the psychotic patient to use the transference depends upon his capacity for symbol formation. This was, I found, at best primitive, if at all, in both the patient and his mother. Moreover, the capability of a junior doctor, even if in personal analysis, to identify and interpret the transference to himself – never mind the patient or anyone else – must be limited, and so have a variable place in this work. Yet it has a place, and it is to be expected that, as the application of psychoanalytic knowledge penetrates further into the culture, it will become more effective. I shall return to this.

8   I was, and remain, thankfully influenced by the work of Lidz and his colleagues at Yale in Connecticut, USA. Lidz's little book *The Family and Human Adaptation* is, in my view, a psychoanalytic classic. Moreover, it protected me from the insistent provocation to act out my own oedipal difficulties. This, in 1964, was very much contrary to the *Zeitgeist*. I was deeply suspicious of the anti-psychiatric and anti-psychoanalytic movement evident in the wilder excesses of the Laing–Cooper 'révolution', wherein all social structure, beginning with the family, came in for destructive criticism. The principle of healing seemed lost to me. Accordingly I tried to reinstate a structure in Villa 21, something akin to the home most of us cherish. This, inevitably, addressed individual feelings in staff quite as much as in patients, and a private life of the patient, staff and the Villa itself was respected and protected.

9   The work and publications of Bruno Bettelheim at the Orthogenic School in Chicago were of initial help to me in setting up and developing some concrete structure to the work of the Villa. It is too easy nowadays to criticise the pioneering work of Bettelheim and others, but for whom our current levels of sophistication would have found no encouragement. The early work begun by Frieda Fromm-Reichmann

and others at Chestnut Lodge, Maryland, USA, was similarly valuable. The unfortunate appellation 'schizophrenogenic mother' had its origin there, a term most effectively trounced as conspicuously uncon-structive, by Hill (1955) in another very helpful publication.

10   Having decided upon the importance of affording patients and nurses consistent and dependable relationships in a 'domestic' setting wherein words could be used to express feelings explicitly, from the outset I endeavoured to place NHS patients in private psychoanalysis! This may sound incredible, but such was my enthusiasm, or naïvety, or both, with the help of Donald Winnicott I got my first patient placed in analysis (Meltzer 1976). Winnicott, though otherwise very encourag-ing, was unenthusiastic about my sending patients out daily to analy-sis. A second and a third patient were placed with Kleinian training analysts. I look back upon this now with astonishment. However, I owe it to Sidney Klein that I was able to recognise that what we were already doing and developing was of fundamental importance. I came subsequently to categorise this work as 'psychoanalytically informed'. It is an epithet which seems to have caught on and become fashionable.

11   I have referred to the way in which the work developed so as to encompass the patient's parents, mother especially. The insistent priva-tion of the mother–son relationship, often sustained and characterised by mutual splitting and projective identification, assured that to address the emotional needs of one without the other was pointless. Moreover, mother would relate to the patient's doctor, and to nobody else. The consultant (S T Hayward) pointed out that it might be expected that the patient's incapacity to use a transference could be paralleled by mother's similar incapability. For the most part, this proved to be true and a psychotherapeutic relationship was sustained conditionally. Mother was not a 'patient'. 'Treatment' was implicit. The 'ill' part of her, the 'mad' part of her, was the patient, in the hospital. That he was held in affection and respected as a young man could astonish mother and permit her to share much of her own life, child-hood and tragedy with the doctor. The degree of separation made possible by this intervention was variable. Seen from the patient's posi-tion, a real interest in mother's emotional predicament assisted in the introjection of a modified good object. As mother felt better about herself and as some good experiences were gathered in the Villa, here and there the overall hopelessness and despair of the patient came to be called in question. Moreover, the nursing staff – and who will say the doctor was not one of them? – came to feel differently and more purposefully about their work and involvement with the patients and each other.

12   Parents came to organise themselves to hold bazaars to raise money for use in the Villa, this, itself, an expression of a more hopeful

and constructive attitude. The only 'result' to which I could point was that if the patient needed to be readmitted, he had not to be psychotic to be so.

13   In the space afforded me I have to limit what can be reported about the Villa 21 experience. This experience is no longer conceivable. Open-ended admission and sojourn in hospital is a thing of the past. Already in the 1960s patients were drugged, discharged, to be repeatedly readmitted in what became known as the revolving door principle. Junior doctors were put on a parallel revolving door called 'rotation', in the interests of 'gaining experience'. It seemed to me that this served to avoid establishing relationships with patients, with nurses, and of patients with nurses. So long as one did not know one could be protected from the pain of knowing the patients were called upon to carry. In order to accomplish anything in life one has to settle down to the task and stop fidgeting.

14   The concept of constructive asylum which I experienced at Shenley Hospital is now a matter of history. But it would be a mistake to deplore change and wring one's hands in despair. It is of the utmost importance in our work to sustain a constructive approach, whatever the obstacles and setbacks. Those at the top, usually the consultant, are entitled to lead, as they earn that entitlement. Foremost will be a capacity to contain one's own as well as the projected despair of staff and patients, and not act it out by projection back as wild analysis. Counter-transference phenomena can, in this area, be most provocative and destructive if not analysed in relation to the transference.

15   The work of mourning, and with it the often painful work of thinking and worrying, is fundamental to any concept of separation and separateness. This is as much true of mother as of her child, of nurse (including doctor) as of the patient. Separation and separateness are not to be confused with physical separation, rejection or abandonment.

16   As Freud called himself a cheerful pessimist, I should say I am an optimist inasmuch as an optimist is one who sees the future is uncertain. But there is a future and it belongs to a younger generation. In the end, we leave behind what we leave in other people, notably our juniors, which is our mutual privilege. The current scene is one of flux, of change everywhere in the world. However, of one thing I am sure, that schizophrenic patients and others will continue to seek safety in that most fundamental hospital, which is in someone's mind. Moreover, that maternal feeling of men and women will always seek to find means to provide it. The chemical pollution of human relationships must ultimately intoxicate those who purvey the drugs in the service of the obliteration of their own pain. It may take a long time; but, in the meanwhile, nurses and doctors seeking to understand their

relationship with themselves and their patients will continue to look to psychoanalysis for help. They are already doing so.

17   Si vis me flere dolendum est
     Primum ipsi tibi

     (If you want me to weep
     You must weep first yourself)

                                        Horace, *Ars Poetica*

Acknowledgement
I acknowledge gratefully the support of my family, my analyst (Tom Hayley), Tom Hayward, the nurses and many others at Shenley in that time.

References
CONRAN, M B (1976a) 'Incestuous failure: studies of transference phenomena with young psychotic patients and their mothers', *International Journal of Psycho-Analysis* 57, pp.477–81

—— (1976b) 'Schizophrenia as incestuous failure. Theoretical implications, derived from transference observations of the young male schizophrenic and his mother, concerning the mother-infant relationship' in J Jørstad & E Ugelstad (eds) *Schizophrenia 75: Proceedings of the fifth International Symposium: Psychotherapy of Schizophrenia*, Oslo, Norway: Universitetsforlaget

—— (1984) 'The patient in hospital', *Psychoanalysis & Psychotherapy*, 1, pp.31–3

—— (1991) 'A note on the nursing relationship', *Psychoanalytic Psychotherapy*, 5, pp.109–14

COOPER, D G (1967) *Psychiatry and Anti-Psychiatry*, Tavistock

HILL, L B (1955) *Psychotherapeutic Intervention in Schizophrenia*, Chicago: University of Chicago Press

LIDZ, T (1963) *The Family and Human Adaptation*, International Psychoanalytical Library no.60, Hogarth Press

MELTZER, D (1976) 'The role of narcissistic organization in communication difficulties of the schizophrenic' in J Jørstad & E Ugelstad (eds) *Schizophrenia 75: Proceedings of the fifth International Symposium: Psychotherapy of Schizophrenia*, Oslo, Norway: Universitetsforlaget

MENZIES, I E P (1960) 'A case-study in the functioning of social systems as a defence against anxiety: a report on a study of the nursing service of a general hospital', *Human Relations*, 13, pp.95–122

REY, J H (1988) 'That which patients bring to analysis', *International Journal of Psycho-Analysis*, 69, pp.457–70

SULLIVAN, H S (1953) *The Interpersonal Theory of Psychiatry*, Tavistock

WINNICOTT, D W (1965) *The Maturation Process and the Facilitating Environment*, Hogarth Press and The Institute of Psycho-Analysis

—— (1968) 'Clinical regression compared with defence organization. Personal communication' in C Winnicott, R Shepherd & M Davis (eds) *Psychoanalytic Explorations*, Karnac Books, 1989

—— (1969) 'The use of an object', *International Journal of Psycho-Analysis*, 50, pp.711–16

3

Michael Sinason

How can you keep your hair on?

Introduction

In common speech, 'keep your hair on' is said to someone when he or she is felt to be in danger of getting into an uncontrolled state of rage. When someone hasn't 'kept their hair on' and there has been an eruption of destructiveness they are often referred to as having gone 'absolutely mad', which recognises how out of contact with reality they are. During the breakdown, the hate, rage and damage is often directed at things that are otherwise particularly cared for and valued. The scale of damage is variable but what is so painful about these situations is that when the individual 'recovers himself' he is usually appalled by what has happened. That is why friends of the individual try to prevent the situation from worsening by saying 'keep your hair on' when they see the early warning signs. They know that the person will regret what they will do if they are taken over by the rage.

These commonplace ways of referring to the nature of a breaking down of mental functioning and its consequences can carry a great wealth of experience of the actual dynamic nature of the processes involved. I think this occurs because people learn an emotional grammar from their interactions with others, which parallels the way they learn to speak. They learn the grammar of mental states from the way that facial expressions and tones of voice change and from the way smaller actions of threatening and gesturing can lead to escalating violence.

Unpacking common knowledge

Once a state of rage has broken out there are different sayings that describe the state. In American slang the epithet 'mad' is accepted as a suitable synonym for angry as in being 'real mad at' someone. The equivalent English phrase is to say that someone is 'hopping mad', which evokes the image of someone so enraged as to be jumping around in a state of aggravated and useless activity. 'Keep your hair on' is an exhortation in response to someone showing early warning signs of developing a state of violent disinhibition. The imagery evoked is

that of someone so enraged that they are yanking their own hair out
by the roots. In saying 'keep your hair on' it is hoped that there is still a
concerned person listening who can feel themselves 'losing it', *ie* losing
touch with reality. The saying is an attempt to forge an alliance with
that person when they are thought to be nearing some point of no
return, after which the option for dialogue will have been removed
and the mad state will have to run its course.

The helplessness of the individual caught up in such states is
illustrated by the phrase 'he was beside himself'. This can be applied to
extreme states of grief as well as rage, but this saying goes beyond
description to provide a visual image of there being two very different
selves existing side by side in a dangerous state of antagonism. Linked
to this is the phrase 'he was not himself', meaning that the extent of
the difference between the 'usual self' and the 'mad self' is so gross
that the differences demand recognition. What is so evocative and
potentially useful about these sayings is that they reveal the state of
being 'oneself' to be vulnerable to being lost or exchanged for being
someone else. After such a take-over the 'usual self' will be so trans-
formed by the state of rage as to be unrecognisable to others.

What makes these transformations so difficult for the 'usual self'
to deal with is that both these selves are felt to be genuine at different
times, but they are enormously different. When in a state of rage, what
is recognised by others as the 'mad self' taking over is felt by the
person experiencing the change as being a necessary and righteous
self-assertion. It is only when the rage abates and the 'usual self'
returns that there can be a shared reality again with the people on
the receiving end of this rage.

Even though there are many such common sayings that illustrate
some knowledge of different selves, fear of these internal processes of
transformation can lead to ill-conceived notions of how to deal with it.
The people who experience the transformation of their usual self and
others who suffer the consequences can try to impose some order on
the situation by deciding 'once and for all' which self is the real or true
one. For example, the victim of an outburst of violent rage can be so
shocked by the scale of the transformation of attitude and behaviour
as to be unable to recognise any longer that there are these two selves.
In these circumstances he might say 'a right bastard he turned out to
be' or 'he showed his true colours'. This is said to indicate that the
'usual self' is now considered to have been a sham and a fake and the
'mad self' is then being designated as the 'real self'. This may happen
in shock or it may arise due to a retaliatory desire to withhold recognition that the person was 'not himself' or was 'beside himself'. This has
the appeal of superficial clarity but dodges entirely the unwelcome
fact that the transformation of one self into another is not under the
elective control of the 'usual self'.

The perceptiveness of these everyday sayings will be illustrated
in this paper by showing how closely they apply to the predicament of

one patient who literally could not 'keep her hair on' because when she was enraged she physically pulled her hair out by the handful. In terms of numbers, public yanking out of hair is extremely rare as a symptom of mental illness, but it is a vivid and appalling image of a state of mind that, if it were loosed upon another individual, would constitute criminal assault. Instead, the damage is wreaked upon the patient's head, producing grievous bodily harm, but of a kind which will not be subject to criminal prosecution. Hair pulling is part of the historic imagery of madness and madhouses through the centuries. The best-known works of art illustrating this are probably Caius Gabriel Cibber's two huge stone figures of madmen named 'Raving and melancholy madness', which surmounted the gates of the New Bethlem Hospital built in Moorfields in 1675, following the Great Fire of London. Patricia Allderidge (1979), the Archivist to the Bethlem Royal Hospital and the Maudsley Hospital, has pointed out the contrast between the dramatic power and pathos of Cibber's figures and the eighteenth-century practice of 'viewing the lunatics' as entertainment for a holiday weekend. Cibber's twin images of helpless mental anguish and hopeless mental vacuity would have made it difficult for the sightseer to be able to mock at insanity without some trepidation. However, the desire to represent the sufferers of mental illness as having brought the state upon themselves overcame such warnings and led to the mocking of the afflicted.

Clinical illustration

The patient I will describe pulled her hair out in front of people in a variety of ways. She came for treatment at the age of 33 years having been referred to me from a psychotherapy clinic to which she had been sent by her GP. The original referral letter said that the patient was someone who 'presents self-inflicted injuries of making herself fat and of pulling out her hair to make herself unattractive'. After she began her sessions, it emerged that she also had some compulsive thoughts which frightened her and which had increased her desire for treatment. If ever she stood on a train platform she became terrified that she would be taken over by the impulse to jump under the train and this was so powerful that she had for some years excluded trains completely as a means of travel. She worked as a sales representative travelling by car to customers to show new products and she had recurrent fantasies of crossing the white line down the centre of the road and having a head-on collision with an oncoming car.

There are many aspects to this patient's character development but I will have to confine myself to those aspects of her life which have, in my view, a bearing on the development of her presenting symptom of pulling her hair out. Her father had schizophrenia and was hospitalised for most of her childhood and he died when the patient was 22 years old. Her mother was well meaning but had a brittle and abrasive personality. My patient rowed incessantly with her mother and they sometimes came to blows. In anger, her mother had said more than once that she had wanted an abortion. Her mother had died just five years after her father. The patient had left school without any exams and worked for the same company for all the subsequent years. She married at 27 but the marriage was regretted within weeks and lasted only a year.

The first memories she had of pulling her hair out were around the age of 17 years. The process involved a form of half-aware twirling and pulling at individual strands that clinically conformed to the adolescent psychiatric disorder termed trichotillomania. This caused sufficient disturbance for her to be taken to her GP, whose response was to tell her that if she carried on she would make herself bald and that she would not have any boyfriends because boys would laugh at her moth-eaten appearance. This supposed confrontation with reality seems to have had little immediate consequence with regard to the symptom, which simply carried on. However, it did have grave consequences for her treatment since it was 16 years before she returned to a different GP in deep depression about the large bald patches she had following episodes of frenetic hair pulling. It was this that led, eventually, to her referral to the psychotherapy clinic. There were a number of different aspects to the hair pulling as she experienced the process and I will quote the patient's own description of these from a session a few weeks after starting.

I do the slow hair pulling when I'm driving or if I'm at home watching the telly. I sort through the hairs one at a time separating each one and smoothing them out and I have no aim to pull any of them out. I don't know I'm doing it half of the time, it's just automatic, but by the end of the day in the car, there are quite a few hairs on the seat. After an evening at home watching telly there is a little pile of hairs on the floor where I've been sitting. After a while of sorting out the hairs I twirl just one single hair around my finger and then when I'm ready I pluck it out. It is very important that it is a single hair and not two and I will go on a long time feeling it to make sure it is only one. People don't really know what I'm doing and I don't want them to notice or say anything about it or it is terrible. I don't like to see the hair on the chairs or on the floor but I can't stop it because I'm usually not aware I'm doing it. If I become aware of it I am usually preoccupied with checking that I have got one hair sorted out and then the whole point is to pull it out, so I can't stop then. But I don't like it and the only way I've been able to stop it for a while is to have my hair cut so short that I can't get a grip on it. I can't twist it round my fingers, so I can't pull it out. But it doesn't help because I spend the whole time feeling it in just the same way to see if it is long enough yet to pull it out. But if someone else is watching me and asks me why I'm doing it or if my Aunt gets angry about it and tells me to stop it, then it is terrible, because then it is different. I feel this hate rise up and I feel myself saying inside: 'right, so you think you can tell me what to do, well I'll show you' and I start pulling it out in twos and threes right in front of them and I want to go on till I'm bald. This makes them go completely spare and they start cursing me and telling me I'm fucking mad and I need locking up somewhere and I feel really pleased. But after a while that fury dies down and then I usually have a look in the mirror to see how big the bald patch is and whether it shows and sometimes I can't believe what I'm seeing, I can't believe that I have done that. I see the bald patch and I know it is going to take three months or so to grow again so it isn't noticed and I burst into tears because I feel so ashamed to go out looking like that.

What is vivid in this description is the completely ruthless determination with which the hair pulling is perpetrated once there is any attempt by anyone to introduce control or to imply that there is something wrong with the milder version. The expression of concern brings about an exhibition of relentless damage that is aimed at establishing the unquestionable mastery of the 'mad self' over the body. The body is treated as a slave whose very life is at the whim of the master. Whilst in this state of mind my patient felt completely identified with the 'mad self' in opposition to whoever it was who had voiced concern and restraint, whether that was a boyfriend, her aunt or a girlfriend. The aim of this demonstration was to punish anyone who had voiced their concern so severely that they would not do it again.

What was even more ghastly for her was the realisation that sometimes this unstoppable cruel exhibition of abuse could be initiated if she herself tried to exercise some restraint in regard to the milder form of hair pulling. She would suddenly then switch internally from being the victim of abuse, concerned about the damage caused, to identifying with the hatred and resentment of the abuser, who is outraged by any attempt at restraint. She would start to think 'right, you think you are going to try and stop me do you, well you are going to have the biggest bald patch ever now and that will show you'. She would then feel pride in the unstoppable nature of the process whereby she was going to be taught a lesson. Then, when she had recovered her 'usual self', she would be devastated by the spectacle of her ruined head, which would take a long time to recover. Each time she went through one of these cycles she became increasingly frightened that the hair roots would eventually cease to be able to recover so that she would be permanently disfigured.

When the identification with the totally dominating and ruthless abuser abates, the patient is left to survey the damage and count the cost and experiences the suffering of being the helpless victim of a callous, psychopathic abuser. The suffering and despair of those periods was enormous and it is not difficult to see why the patient returned repeatedly to her thoughts of 'white lining'. This meant, for her, a final head-on collision with the abuser, in which abused and abuser would both meet in a deadly mutual revenge. The fact that there might be occupants in the other vehicle who were unaware of this desperate internal drama and yet might lose their lives in this final internal confrontation did not enter into her reckoning. The fact that she would lose her life in such a final confrontation did, however, disturb her and played an important part in her seeking help.

In the sessions, the nature of this patient's internal predicament presented itself in ways other than hair pulling at first. What happened was that if there was a session in which she had been telling me a lot about her life and some progress was being made in under-standing, in the following session she would be rendered silent. She would tell me that she couldn't think of anything to say and would then pick her nails, twiddle with her hair or look around the room with an absolute certainty that there would be no words forthcoming on that day. The session was in effect yanked out by the roots with the implacable ruthlessness that characterised her violent hair-pulling episodes. When this pattern had been repeated many times so that there was no doubt about the sequence, we could both see that the silence had all the heavyweight absolutism in stopping her life from developing that was also evident in the hair pulling.

Towards the end of the first year there was another vivid encounter with her ferocious 'mad self' which showed that hair pulling was but one string to the bow of this disordered self. When she had come to the preliminary meeting with me she was substantially overweight. As she became more involved in the analytic work she decided that she would go on a diet. The outstanding feature of this diet was that she found it no trouble at all! Previously any diet was thrown out with the first deviation because it was imposed with the same absolutism that suffused her hair pulling. Under this regime, a deviation of some kind would be inevitable and any deviation resulted in a total demolition of the diet and its replacement by bulimic stuffing. This would only end when either she felt she was going to be sick or when there was nothing left in her house to eat. This time, however, the diet was imposed with the same conditions, but she did not deviate at all and she began to shed weight by the stone.

Concurrent with the return from obesity towards an ordinary body weight she began to dress in much more elegant and feminine styles of clothing and she began to talk about stopping coming to her sessions, because the excess weight had been one of the main reasons for seeking treatment. This process took many months to evolve and I knew I was being handed a ready-made opportunity to collude and duck the arduous analysis that lay ahead. The prospect of having to face the full force of the illness I did not relish any more than she did. But I knew that the lack of internal opposition to these changes was not consistent with what we both knew of the nature of the tyranny of these states. I therefore talked to her of the silent sessions and how we knew from them of the opposition that existed within her to a fuller understanding of her problems from the analysis. The implication was therefore that the move to diet her down to a weight which might persuade her to leave was under the influence of the dominating, hair-pulling self, which was using that as the means to silence the analysis and yank it out of her life.

In the session in which I interpreted the situation in these terms she could barely believe that I was saying such things. She had been absolutely convinced that I would take her view that she must be better now since she was looking so much better than she had for years. She had become quite convinced that the reason she had come to me for help was for the purpose of losing weight and that since that was now accomplished she could not see the point in continuing. She said that she had not forgotten the matter of her hair pulling but that there had not been any violent episodes recently and it was growing all right again. She said she was much less bothered about that now than her weight, which was itself obviously all right. She was so sure that I would want to be rid of her psychopathic 'mad self' the way she desperately wanted to be rid of it, she could not believe that I was not taking the opportunity to do so. She thought I would be pleased with the changes I saw and would be congratulating myself for being a good therapist and to encourage this she told me how, in fact, people at work had been saying how amazed they were at the changes.

However, when her hair-pulling 'mad self' realised that the attempt to silence both my patient and me had not worked, there was an enormous eruption of rage. My patient was set upon in a paroxysm of hair pulling and food stuffing which left her 4 stone heavier than she had ever been before and with large bald patches on her head which were easily visible from where I sat. However, she continued to be both astonished and deeply grateful for my willingness to be an ally to her in dealing with that ferocious illness and she dedicated herself to the analytic task with me through thick and thin during the succeeding six years.

The treatment was twice weekly for the first two years and then increased to three and then to four sessions per week for the last two years. The difficulties should not be underestimated. What the analysis allowed was the progressive mapping of ways in which the arrogant, controlling and domineering 'mad self' could permeate throughout the fabric of her life. Her money, for example, could be spent with thought and planning or could be spent bulimically in a credit card binge. This left her having to count the cost in hours of overtime work, to pay off the debt. Similarly, her time could be spent thinking about places to go for holidays or new job opportunities, or instead she could find herself enslaved to a work schedule imposed by her 'mad self' that left no time at all for life beyond work. Her friendships, male and female, could have in them profound wishes for involvement and interest or could be taken over by a mind that was callously indifferent to the individuality of the people concerned.

In the early years of the treatment she experienced enormous frustration at not being able to grasp thoughts physically. She would say exasperatedly that the only things that she could understand were things that she could get her hands round and squeeze. Since my words were not like that she couldn't possibly see how I expected her to understand them! She was therefore quite unable to think about the content of anything I said and tended to deal with it entirely in terms of whether it made her feel good or made her feel bad. She could not think about the pros and cons of decisions that faced her or evaluate options because, to the ruthless, hair-pulling 'mad self', thinking was simply a time-wasting activity. If you wanted something or wanted to be rid of something you simply shoved it in or yanked it out. In this bulldozing approach to life, decision-making is governed solely by the pleasure–pain principle. If it feels good do it, if it feels bad don't do it!

The move from concrete symbolic equations (Segal 1957) to true symbolic functioning is not, however, brought about by either 'crying over' or 'decrying' the takeover of the patient's mind by that of the 'mad self'. What is needed is that the patient recognises the conceptual impoverishment and detachment from reality of the mind of the 'mad self'. Each exploration of the problem of differentiating 'who is who' internally, in a new physical context, brings new aspects of the matter into the realms of thought. What is grasped in one setting can then begin to function as a metaphor for understanding the problem in another context. Thus she became able to talk about a 'hair-pulling attitude' to spending money or to sexual life. This new metaphoric capacity moves the patient gradually away from seeing the 'mad self' as a true representative of herself. The 'mad self' can then be recognised as an 'other' self with a very restricted ability to relate to the interpersonal world. With patience and hard work a genuine interest in this 'other' self can be fostered to replace the attitudes of confrontation and condemnation which so exacerbate and inflame the problem.

Without this shift in attitude to the internal 'other' the faculties of consideration and judgement in interpersonal life are compromised because they are not applied consistently internally and externally. In fact, the patient's progress in the later parts of the analysis can be measured, quite accurately, by the degree to which there is a genuine interest and concern to understand the reasons why this 'other' becomes disturbed and tries to take over control of the patient's life.

Co-existing selves

The gradual elucidation of the reasons for the existence of completely different co-existing selves is a long and difficult task. Sinason (1993) and Richards (1999) have reviewed different psychoanalytic conceptualisations that are available to understand this, and Jenkins (1999) shows how the existence of a 'psychotic self' cohabiting with a 'non-psychotic self' can be seen in many differing psychopathologies. Any notions of modifying or integrating this 'mad self' through therapy are ignoring the evidence that this self does not learn from experience and cannot change in any way. In contrast, the 'usual self' is the potential partner in the therapeutic alliance with the analyst or therapist. Changes that occur do so only within the understanding and capabilities of the patient's 'usual self'. The 'mad self' continues to influence the patient, although less so when the patient can anticipate and understand the reasons this other self is so disturbed. A genuine treatment alliance cannot be expected at the outset of treatment, even though it might appear so. This is because the transactions between patient and analyst are filtered through a censorship system operated through 'internal advice' to the patient from his or her 'mad self'.

When someone has been 'beside themselves' the recovery of their 'usual self' usually takes a few hours or, at most, a day or so. The return journey can be somewhat precarious, however, since there is often humiliation and shame to be negotiated about what has been said or done whilst the individual was out of touch. It is humiliating because the behaviour can often be very far removed indeed from the sort of things that would be usually done. The 'usual self' is therefore in the invidious position of making amends for actions taken when he is 'not himself'. If there is too much condemnation, the patient's own knowledge that he was 'not himself' is likely to become muddled up with a new bout of righteous self-assertion of the 'mad self' and result in another outbreak of rage. If the frequency or duration of these states increases significantly, and particularly if the recovery is incomplete, then the patient may be sliding into what will eventually be recognised as mental illness. Martin Jenkins (1999) has explored many different diagnostic groups in which these internal 'take-overs' by the 'mad self' constitute the central feature in the evolution of the illness.

A difficulty that can arise when someone first comes to a professional to seek help is that guilt or shame can drive the individual to try to take premature responsibility for the destructive state of mind. This can sometimes be mirrored by a desire in the professional to see any references by the patient to damage being caused by some 'other self' as simply a desire to evade responsibility. Any such urgency in the therapist to allocate responsibility is picked up immediately by the patient, who will pay lip service to the idea that they are 'responsible for their actions'. However, they actually know that this is impossible, since they wouldn't be coming for help if the process were under their control. This premature claiming of responsibility is invariably under the influence of the 'mad self' and forms a very effective way of stopping the recognition of the near-total autonomy that the 'mad self' has. Genuine responsibility can only be achieved when the processes that bring about the switch of selves are understood. Then the freedom of the 'mad self' to have his or her own way, is more limited.

The actual formal category of mental illness that emerges when someone is breaking down depends on the interaction of genetic predisposition to particular mental disorders with personal identifications with significant people. My patient's hair-pulling 'mad self' was as ferocious, when disturbed, as any schizophrenic, including her father. By her account, her father was very sensible and gentle unless stressed by some argument, when he would start talking what she called 'rubbish'. My patient's 'mad self' was also more callous and cruel in its determination to dominate than her mother had ever been. When aroused, this self had the arrogance and brittle narcissism that is the hallmark of what is known in psychoanalysis as narcissistic character pathology, and which has been described by Rosenfeld (1987) and Bion (1967). This type of character ranges insensibly from the touchy hypersensitivities and egoisms of everyday life at one end of the spectrum, while at the other end it blurs into what Freud called the narcissistic neuroses and which are now called the psychoses.

My patient, however, had her own self who brought her for help and sustained her through difficult times so that she might find a way out of the trap of cyclical abuse. The growth of her own 'usual self' had been helped by her mother's sister, who had, on occasion, looked after her with concern and clear thinking. My patient hated lying and evasion and was reliable and sincere in her dealings with people, and this was reflected in the way she had stayed working in the same company for years. In six years of therapy and then analysis she was never late or absent from sessions and she worked hard to earn enough to pay for the treatment. This had links with the way that her mother also worked hard to look after the fundamentals of life in providing a home, food and clothes. These character strengths were built on during the analysis to equip her gradually with enough understanding to shift the internal situation so that she could look after her 'mad self' with concern, rather than having that self repeatedly taking over and sidelining her, in a ruthless way.

The nature, extent and the frequency of mental and behavioural disturbances during mental illness will all influence the diagnostic assessment. But it is remarkable what a high threshold of acceptance there is in ordinary social life for serious personal damage or actual bodily damage. Thus an individual has to be subjected to the most extreme abuses of over-eating or under-eating before it is recognised as a problem, and sometimes even at 'death's door' the seriousness of the problem is not acknowledged. Self-mutilation of various kinds such as wrist slashing or thigh slashing usually obtains earlier recognition as a mental illness problem. Overdoses, however, are often minimised and the mutilating injuries that can be the result of being 'beside yourself' while at the wheel of a car or on a motor-bike are usually not counted at all as being part of the spectrum of mental illness.

When the patient I have reported was 17 years, her trichotillomania was viewed by her GP as a foolishness that he tried to shame her out of by telling her she wouldn't have boyfriends. By the time she was 33, a different GP saw the symptom as abnormal enough to refer her to a psychotherapy clinic. However, he did not recognise how out of control her problem was since he referred to her behaviour as 'making herself unattractive'. In these circumstances I think it is legitimate to ask 'how could she keep her hair on'? It was only the persistence and worsening extent of the physical damage she was suffering which became her credentials for needing psychological help.

It is impossible to know whether she would ever have developed a schizophrenic illness, like her father, if she had not come into treatment. Her difficulties corresponded to the diagnostic category of 'impulsive' or 'borderline psychotic' personality disorder, a condition which is usually associated with acts of self-harm. Over a 15-year period approximately 10% of borderline personality disorder patients will have committed suicide (Swartz et al 1990). I think that the chances of this patient crossing the white line while driving, in cataclysmic confrontation with her illness, would have been very high if she had not found a way to mitigate the scale of internal domination and abuse she was subjected to.

References

ALLDERIDGE, P (1979) ' Caius Gabriel Cibber: figures from the gates of Bedlam, c. 1676', *Bethlem & Maudsley Gazette*, Spring, pp.10–14

BION, W (1967) *Second Thoughts: selected papers on psychoanalysis*, Maresfield Reprints, 1984

JENKINS, M (1999) 'Clinical application of the concept of internal cohabitation', *British Journal of Psychotherapy*, 16(1), pp.27–42

RICHARDS, J (1999) 'The concept of internal cohabitation' in S Johnson & S Ruszczynski (eds) *Psychoanalytic Psychotherapy in the Independent Tradition*, Karnac Books

ROSENFELD, H (1987) *Impasse and Interpretation*, Tavistock

SEGAL, H (1957) 'Notes on symbol formation' in *The Work of Hanna Segal*, New York: Jason Aronson, pp.49–65

SINASON, M (1993) 'Who is the mad voice inside?', *Psychoanalytic Psychotherapy*, 7 (3), pp.207–21

SWARTZ, M & BLAZER D G et al (1990) 'Estimating the prevalence of borderline personality disorder in the community', *Journal of Personality Disorders*, 4(3), pp.257–272

Note

This paper was first given as a lecture for the Institute of Psycho-Analysis Public Lecture Day on Psychosis on 13 May 1989 and was revised for a repeat on 19 May 1990. It was further revised for a lecture on 3 November 1990 at the West Midlands Institute of Psychotherapy, Birmingham. It was revised and re-written for publication 15 February 1999.

4

Thomas Freeman

The delusions of the non-remitting schizophrenias: parallels with childhood phantasies

M Bleuler's (1978) follow-up studies have confirmed the clinical observation that the course of the illness in non-remitting schizophrenias is towards the establishment of relatively stable 'end states'. The term 'end state' as used by M Bleuler (1978) does not mean that the process of illness has come to an end, is incapable of further development for good or ill, or that further changes may not affect the personality. Only when the illness has continued in this relatively steady condition for five years can it be designated an 'end state'. Although acute attacks may occur during 'end states' they are ephemeral and there is a return to the quiescent condition. M Bleuler distinguishes three types of 'end state': severe, moderately severe and mild. Dementia and defect state were the terms used in past times to describe the first two. The third type consists of those patients whose illness is not immediately obvious, who can conduct a rational conversation without the intrusion of delusional and hallucinatory experiences and can undertake useful work. The delusions which occur during the initial, acute attack of a schizophrenic psychosis are inclined to disappear along with other acute manifestations (E Bleuler 1911). In contrast the delusions which make their appearance when the illness follows a chronic course (non-remitting) tend to persist unchanged over many years (E Bleuler 1911). The introduction of drug therapy has not altered this apart from causing a transient disappearance of the delusions. The long-term observation of schizophrenic patients whose illnesses have reached 'end states' suggests that the content of the delusions is different from that present during the initial attack. The delusions to be described here are drawn from 12 cases, four of which had reached a severe 'end state' (three women and one man), six had reached a moderately severe 'end state' (four women and two men), and two, a mild 'end state' (one man and one woman). The retrieval of the delusions was sometimes easy, but occasionally very arduous. The greatest difficulty was encountered when there was inattention, withdrawal and cognitive disorganisation. The presence of thought-blocking, derailment of speech, the inappropriate use of words (loss of the symbolic, function), aberrant concepts (Schilder 1923) and neologisms combined to conceal the content of delusions (Freeman 1969). Perseverations, transitivistic phenomena and appersonations expressed in speech contributed to the confusion caused by the breakdown of syntax. The recovery of delusions in such severe 'end states' can therefore only be accomplished piecemeal. Fortunately there are occasions, however brief, when speech regains its communicative function and a detail of the patient's delusional reality makes its appearance. These are occasions when the patient has a pressing need or is angry because of a disappointment (Freeman 1969). Although patients whose illness has reached a mild 'end state' can communicate verbally when they so desire, it is unusual for them immediately to reveal the details of their delusions. The reticence tends to disappear when they discern that an interest is being taken in their circumstances. After some weeks, however, a reluctance to continue with daily sessions begins to appear. Patients fear that they are wasting the psychiatrist's time. Then they either stop attendance or become increasingly withdrawn. The psychiatrist may be accused of exerting a malevolent influence. Such a sequence of events occurs despite the chemotherapy. After a few weeks it is sometimes possible to re-engage patients in further meetings. However, after a short while the reluctance and withdrawal appear once more.

Common to the 12 patients were, delusions whose content consisted of wishes fulfilled. A male patient (severe 'end state') claimed that he had found the hospital in ruins and had restored it. Another male patient (moderate 'end state') believed that he had invented machines of inestimable value to society; another man (moderately severe 'end state') that he had uncovered a criminal conspiracy to destroy the world. The wish phantasies of the female patients were of a romantic–erotic nature (see Bleuler 1911). The delusional phantasies of the mild and moderately severe 'end states' were internally consistent and constant. Erotic phantasies were also found in male patients. The beloved, in both male and female patients, was usually known either before or shortly after the onset of the illness. In severe 'end states' the erotic phantasies were ephemeral and fragmentary. The lovers who appeared miraculously in the night had never been known. In every case the patients blame persecutors for their being deprived of the fruits of their achievements and of their lovers. Persecutors had caused them to be confined in hospitals or placed in hostels. Those enemies were often known to the patients. Sometimes it was the parents who were blamed but many patients denied their parentage. Their real parents were persons of importance. As has been described, these complaints did not necessarily lead to anger but they could do so, as will be illustrated below. The delusional reality in some cases has a distinctive feature. In two of the female patients, one having reached a severe 'end state', there was an imaginary person (a 'delusional object') who played an important part in the patient's life. In the first case the imaginary figure was a male teacher at the school the patient had attended as a child. He talked to her. Sometimes he was complimentary, at other times critical. She looked to him for advice. She said, 'Mr X (the teacher) does not allow me to speak to them [the other patients] ... he asks if I am being polite.' During meetings with this patient, there were occasions when she appeared to be playing the part of the schoolmaster, or the writer was allocated this role.

In the second case the imaginary figure was a woman doctor. The discovery of this 'delusional object' occurred unexpectedly when the patient was sought out after a break in the daily meetings which had been going on for at least three months. She did not want to speak and shouted angrily, 'I don't like you, you don't follow me, I only like my own doctor.' Enquiry eventually revealed that this doctor had been the family practitioner but the patient had not seen her for many years. Her 'doctor' assumed full responsibility for her. She told her when to wash, when to shampoo her hair, change her clothes, when to eat and when to go to the lavatory. These hallucinated instructions explained her frequently occurring active and aggressive negativism. The wish delusions of 'end states' were not in evidence during the initial, acute attacks of the illness. At the onset the delusional ideas were predominantly persecutory. Many patients believed that perverse sexuality or promiscuous tendencies were being imposed upon them by persecutors, known or unknown. These delusional ideas disappeared after the first or second relapse. A case in point is that of a young man who believed that others regarded him as a homosexual. Following a remission which lasted about eight months he fell ill again. This time there was no longer any concern about homosexuality. Instead he was preoccupied with thoughts about a girl he believed was in love with him. He accused his parents of hospitalising him to prevent him seeing the girl. This delusion (erotomania) became part of a more complex psychotic reality which developed as time passed. Inherent in the delusional reality of 'end states' is omnipotence and control. Any event or experience which runs counter to the omnipotent phantasies is denied. Delusional ideas of this kind are the counterpart of 'passivity' experiences. The polarity – controlling and being controlled – is derived from the observation that patients who in 'end states' claim such powers are those who complained of passivity experiences in their first attacks. For example, a male patient whose first attack had been characterised by passivity experiences claimed, when his illness reached an 'end state' (moderately severe), that he had detected the existence of master criminals who secretly, and unbeknown to their victims, caused them to carry out robberies and murders for their own gain: 'They move them about like puppets,' he said. He was immune to their influence, although they were forever trying to gain control over him.

It is usual for acute attacks of short duration to occur during 'end states' (M Bleuler 1978). Persecutory ideas, hallucination, withdrawal, agitation and negativism may constitute the symptomatology. Such acute phases occurring during 'end states' have, as their immediate causes, affects provoked by changes in routine, by real or unreal expectations and disappointments (E Bleuler, 1911). When patients are seen on a regular basis, an opportunity is afforded of witnessing the stimulus which leads to these acute episodes. The fact that patients in 'end states' believe that their wishes have been fulfilled leads to expectations which in the nature of things cannot be met. A male patient (severe 'end state') believed that he was owed large sums of money. Once given the money he would marry the girl who he believed loved him. When this man was asked to participate in regular meetings he readily agreed. Only later did it become apparent that the willingness arose from the expectation that the writer could get the money for him. After several months of daily meetings, he became withdrawn and negativistic. At first sight there was no apparent cause for this reaction. Later, however, he berated the writer, accusing him of failing to keep his promise to get him the money. A female patient (mild 'end state') refused to leave the house because she heard a neighbour calling her a prostitute. She had recently been in hospital for a minor operation, where she met a man who, she concluded, found her attractive. This information was revealed only reluctantly.

There is agreement that the delusional reality of established, cases of schizophrenia is in the nature of a substitute for material reality (E Bleuler 1911; S Freud 1911; 1924). This theory implies that the wish delusions compensate for and protect against an external reality which is viewed to be dangerous and frustrating. Regarded in this way the wish delusions reinforce the protection initially provided by the break with reality which E Bleuler (1911) described as the negative element of autism and S Freud (1911) as the withdrawal of object cathexis. Despite this, patients in 'end states' are not spared bouts of 'persecutory anxiety' in the manner already described. This reveals that the wish delusions which form the nucleus of the psychotic reality are by themselves unable constantly to maintain the defence against the dangers evoked by the derivatives of instinct. It is the protective or defensive use of wish delusions which led Anna Freud (1936) to compare them with certain kinds of childhood phantasy. The similarities extend beyond content to sources and manner of formation. Some children employ phantasies to relieve objective anxiety and pain (A Freud 1936). A child's fear that his jealousy and envy of the father will lead to retribution initiates a series of unconscious mental events (displacement, reversal) designed to dispel objective anxiety. A dangerous animal substitutes for the frightening father and, its nature changed, becomes a friend and protector over whom the child has

complete control. This substitution also occurs during the psychoanalytical treatment of children when fear of the father, arising from the
projection of the child's hostility, is displaced on to the person of the
analyst. To ward off fear of the analyst the child makes use of toys and
imaginary figures to protect him and control the analyst. In the case of
objective pain, the child's sense of helplessness *vis-à-vis* the parents is
removed by removing the true nature of things. Denial of reality is
achieved through wishful phantasies in which the child assumes
directly or through the medium of imaginary figures the power and
strength of the father whom he both fears and loves. The control over
the father – which the child gains through wish phantasies – is no
different in nature to the omnipotence and omniscience which is at
the core of the wishful delusions of patients in 'end states'. Children
also make use of wish phantasies to deny real, distressing events (A
Freud 1973). The father of a little boy, Bertie, aged four and a half, was
killed in an air-raid (A Freud 1973). In the weeks following this tragic
event he repeatedly talked of his father as alive. His father had gone off
to work in his raincoat and hat because it was raining. When he did
not return Bertie said that he put on his coat and went to look for him.
After finding him he brought him home. This phantasy of rescuing the
father had further expression in a phantasy of being the driver of a
fire-engine. He put out fires, rescued people and took them quickly to
the doctor. In a game in which he built houses and knocked them
down with marbles, representing bombs, all the people were saved.
This outcome was in contrast to other children who, playing a similar
game, said the people were killed. Bertie's game had the purpose of
denying what had happened in reality: the death of his father in an
air-raid. Its compulsive nature betrayed the fact that the denial was
becoming less successful (A Freud 1973). This little boy's phantasy in
which he omnipotently restored the houses and saved the people is
identical to that of the chronically ill schizophrenic patient who
claimed that he had rebuilt the hospital and restored the inmates to
health after the hospital had been destroyed.

A similar sequence of mental events is to be found in patients
who fall ill with a maniacal illness following a bereavement or a disappointment in love. Denial of the loss of the love object is achieved by
wish phantasies replacing reality. The love object has not gone away
and in proof of this the patient insists that he has seen him or her, or
has heard their voice. Other patients, nurses and doctors are
misidentified as the lost love object. These wish delusions disappear
with the remission of the maniacal attack. However, they become
permanent in the mental life of schizophrenic patients whose illness
was initially precipitated by the loss of a real love object. A young
woman in her early twenties was jilted by her fiancé. After some
months she came to believe that her former fiancé was trying to
contact her. Her belief that enemies were preventing them from
coming together led to her hospitalisation. After two periods of

partial remission the illness entered into a chronic stage (moderately severe 'end state') which was characterised by short-lived bouts of persecutory ideas. At the centre of the psychotic reality was the delusion that she was married and had a son. Her husband was a doctor. She had met him in one of the hospitals in which she was a patient. The doctor had taken the place of her former fiancé. She claimed that the family solicitor had a box in his possession which contained her marriage certificate and a boy's suit. She and her husband had had to separate because of her family's disapproval and opposition. Her brother had recently introduced her to a young man whom he encouraged to make sexual advances to her. She knew that her husband was constantly trying to get in touch with her but he was prevented from doing so by her mother and brother.

There is another type of childhood phantasy which has a relevance for the psychotic reality of schizophrenic patients. This is the imaginary companion (Sperling 1954; Nagera 1969) and the phantasy of having a twin (Burlingham 1952). Imaginary companions occur in children between the ages of two and a half and three, and between nine and ten. In some cases the phantasy persists into adolescence and there have been reports of it continuing into adult life. In contrast to other childhood phantasies the imaginary companion occupies a physical space in the child's world. It has a special intensity and vividness. The content of the child's interaction with his or her imaginary companion – what the companion says, how the child responds and how he perceives the companion – has led to the following conclusions (Nagera 1969). In young children the companion's help is required for the control of wishes and needs which would lead to conflict with the parents (external conflict). This assists the process of internalisation of restraints on 'instinct'. In older children the companion acts as a 'prop' for the newly emergent super-ego. The companion can express those wishes and actions which are unacceptable to the child. Here the companion is blamed by the child for actions he undertook and for which he has been criticised. The companion may therefore come to play the role of scapegoat. In his study of the imaginary companion, Nagera (1969) has drawn attention to the fact that the companion makes his or her appearance when children feel lonely, neglected or rejected. Thus the birth of a sibling is often the occasion for the emergence of the imaginary companion. However, a companion may appear when children are confronted with real object-loss or suffer when they feel threatened by their helplessness to influence the behaviour of adults. It is in these instances that the phantasy of the imaginary companion or twin acts as a protection and a defence. Sperling (1954) describes the case of a boy of four who would only speak and act if his imaginary companion, Rudiman, gave permission. Rudiman was taller and stronger than his father. His voice was so loud that the boy had to cover his ears when he spoke. This imaginary companion allowed the child to sustain the illusion that he was independent and free of his father's control. In this way reality was reversed and denied. In common with other companions, however, Rudiman would be blamed for encouraging 'anti-social' acts.

Delusional figures analogous to imaginary companions are periodically found in long-standing cases of schizophrenia. The delusional object, like the imaginary companion, may act as an external authority and guide and, like Rudiman (Sperling 1954), give the patient the illusion of being independent of the requirements of the nursing staff. The delusional object is never blamed for unwanted speech or action, as happens when persecutors, known or unknown persons, are blamed for 'passivity' experiences. There was nothing to suggest, in the two cases described earlier, that the delusional objects had imaginary companions as childhood precursors. Such a psychopathological development was encountered, however, in a woman patient aged 34 who was hospitalised on account of an acute psychotic attack characterised by auditory hallucinations. The patient was married with two children. She complained of a female voice in her head. The voice instructed her to act in a manner which caused her great distress. The voice told her to strike her husband and throw tea over a newly painted wall. The voice instructed her not to speak, told her to sit still or go for a walk. It also criticised her appearance, commented on her actions and recalled painful memories of childhood. She became frightened when the voice told her to kill herself. The patient said, at first, that she had become aware of the voice in her head when she suspected that her husband was showing an excessive interest in her sister, who was separated from her husband. She asked her husband to promise not to have any contact with her. After some time she discovered that he was indeed having an affair with her sister. The voice had already been telling her that this was so, and it reminded her of actions which indicated that he no longer loved her. The voice encouraged her to act violently toward him. She became fearful lest she might give way to those provocations and kill her husband. During regular meetings with the writer she recalled that as a very young child, the youngest of three children, she had been extremely close to her mother. Later this changed, and this, according to the patient, was due to a serious deterioration in her home. This led to bitter rows between the parents with the husband accusing his wife of infidelity. The patient felt alone and neglected. When she was approximately eight or nine years of age an imaginary companion appeared on the scene. The companion, a girl somewhat older than herself, comforted her when she was lonely. They talked together and played games. The companion reassured her when she felt afraid at night. Sometimes, however, the companion would make her afraid, telling her to frighten her mother by running away from home or encouraging her to bang her head against the wall. The companion remained with her until she was about 16. At this time she began to make friends for the first time, and as these friendships developed the companion faded and disappeared. When, at the age of 20, she met her husband, she felt that at last she had found someone in whose life she would be first. As memories of her disappointment in her husband returned, she recalled that when she discovered he was losing interest in her, the imaginary companion returned to comfort and console her. However, within a short time the companion began to criticise the husband and remind the patient of his shortcomings. Imperceptibly (or so it seemed to the patient in retrospect), the image of the companion faded, leaving only the disembodied voice whose utterances were described above. In this case the 'persecutory voice' developed out of the imaginary companion. The hatred which the patient unconsciously felt for her husband was attributed to the new version of the companion, in much the same way as the young child regards his companion as the source of all those wishes which he has come to fear. In childhood this patient's imaginary companion became the focus of the libidinal cathexes withdrawn from a mother perceived as rejecting. In adult life, it came to act as a vehicle for aggression, as it had done, on occasions, in childhood.

The young child's use of wish fantasies to deny an unacceptable reality is an aspect of normal ego development (A Freud 1936). Young children can reconcile the contradictions which exist between the psychical reality afforded by wishes and material reality. This is true in the case of imaginary companions. However, such contradictions become untenable as reality testing increasingly establishes itself. This is not to say that wish fantasies are no longer evoked to soften the impact of dissapointment, frustrations and object loss, but they make no impact on the way the individual perceives himself and others (S Freud 1916). As Anna Freud (1936) says, 'the original importance of the day-dream as a means of defending against objective anxiety is lost when the earliest period of childhood comes to an end'.

The psychotic reality of patients whose schizophrenic illnesses have reached 'end-states' reveals that, like small children, they are not dismayed by the fact that the reality created by their wishes cannot be reconciled with external reality. It is the existence of the two realities, as in the phenonomen of double book-keeping, which led Bleuler (1911) to suggest that 'systematic splitting' is the characteristic clinical feature of the schizophrenias.

At first sight it would appear as if the psychotic reality has resulted solely from the emergence of a childhood mode of mental activity (denial in fantasy) which is no longer appropriate and adaptive (Hughlings Jackson 1894). However, wish fantasies are freely employed to counter frustrations and dissappointments in both the healthy and those who suffer from symptom and other character neuroses (see S Freud 1916, and his concept of introversion). It may be that the measures employed to counter objective pain (A Freud 1936) – measures of displacement or reversal – are predominant elements of the defence organisation of the pre-illness personality of those whose schizophrenias proceed to 'end-states'. It is patients such as these whose pre-psychotic personalities are often described as schizoid–pathological (Bleuler 1978). Omnipotence – overt or covert – is a feature of such personalities. Could this omnipotence be the result of a heightened sensitivity to perceptions which evoke objective pain?

The fact that wish fantasies exist and act defensively, as they can do, indicates that their content has been successfully disconnected from wishes which evoke anxiety. Clinical work with young children and schizophrenic patients has shown that these protective wish fantasies can be swept aside and replaced by anxiety. A girl aged four, who was undergoing psychoanalytic treatment, was able to deny her phsysical immaturity *vis-à-vis* her mother by means of a pregnancy fantasy. A chronically ill schizophrenic patient denied his 'incarceration' in the hospital by means of the delusion that he controlled the routine of the institution. When the child patient and the adult schizophrenic patient became anxious the defensive phantasies disappeared. The little girl feared that she might harm the analyst with the flatus she passed during the session. This reflected her unconscious wish to destroy her love object with faeces. The schizophrenic patient dreaded that, in the course of defecating, he had generated a wind which had destroyed the countryside. These pregenital wish phantasies are clearly of a different order from those which serve defensive aims. This replacement of the latter by the former may be observed in psychotherapeutic work with established cases of schizophrenia and during the psychoanalytical treatment of young children. The reversal mechanism no longer operates, leaving the patient with the perception of the psychiatrist or analyst as hostile or dangerous. A female schizophrenic patient engaged in psychotherapy responded with an erotomanic delusion: that the psychiatrist was in love with her, was going to marry her and give her a child. After some weeks she refused further meetings, accusing the psychiatrist of secretly giving her a drug which rendered her helpless and raping her. He had infected her with syphilis and aborted her pregnancy. It would appear, therefore, that in the case of the schizophrenias which reach 'end states', defensive wish phantasies will only maintain themselves as long as interpersonal contacts which provoke the arousal of dangerous wish phantasies can be avoided.

References

BLEULER, E (1911) *Dementia Praecox*, New York: Int. University Press, 1951

BLEULER, M (1978) *The Schizophrenic Disorders*, New Haven: Yale University Press

BURLINGHAM, D (1952) *Twins*, Imago

FREEMAN, T (1969) *Psychopathology of the Psychoses*, Tavistock

FREUD, A (1936) *The Ego and the Mechanisms of Defence*, Hogarth Press

—— (1973) *Infants Without Families and Reports on the Hampstead Nurseries 1939–45*, Hogarth Press

FREUD, S (1911) 'Psycho-analytic notes on an autobiographical account of a case of paranoia', S.E.12

—— (1916) *Introductory Lectures on Psycho-Analysis*, S.E.16

—— (1924) 'The loss of reality in neurosis and psychosis', S.E.19

HUGHLINGS JACKSON, J (1894) 'The factors of insanities' in *Selected Writings*, Vol. 2, New York: Basic Books

NAGERA, H (1969) 'The imaginary companion', *Psychoanalytic Study of the Child*, 24, pp.165–96

SCHILDER, P (1923) *Medical Psychology*, New York: Int. University Press, 1951

SPERLING, O (1954) 'An imaginary companion, representing a pre-stage of the superego', *Psychoanalytic Study of the Child*, 9, pp.252–88

5

Richard Lucas

Managing psychotic patients in a day hospital setting

Introduction

The psychiatric day hospital can be regarded as one form of a therapeutic community. Maxwell Jones, a pioneer of the therapeutic community, described this as being a 'living/learning' situation, both for staff and patients (Jones 1952). However, there is nothing magical about a therapeutic community; it is only as effective as the sum of its input – by both staff and patients. In this paper I want to concentrate on the role of the day hospital in the management of psychotic patients, especially in attempting to make emotional contact with those in seemingly inaccessible states, through the utilisation of analytic insights. Illustrative clinical examples will be given, related to the day hospital setting

General psychiatric approach

The general psychiatric approach to psychosis does not usually incorporate a space for analytic thinking. General psychiatrists look on schizophrenia in terms of an organic disorder for which we have not as yet fully identified the cause, but which drugs (major tranquillisers) help. For example, in a review on the current management of schizophrenia, on the role of psychotherapeutic input, Fahy and David write 'Psychotherapy, both individual and family, continues to fight a rearguard action against exclusively pharmacological treatment of schizophrenia' (Fahy & David 1993). Diagnosis is made by trying to be objective about describing subjective experiences (Jaspers phenomenological approach). Some symptoms are said to be more important in making the diagnosis: first rank symptoms, *eg* hearing voices commenting in the third person, and primary delusions. These features are elicited by the mental state examination. A social history is taken, including when the patient last worked, and whether they have been able to mix with others or have always been withdrawn – the so-called schizoid personality. Also the family atmosphere is assessed. It is known that, apart from stopping medication, an over-pressuring home atmosphere with unrealistic high expectations (high expressed emotion) is a major cause of relapse (Gelder *et al* 1990). However, while all this is relevant in making a diagnosis and assessing social and family stresses linked with relapses, in my view we then need to make a further mental state assessment – a psychoanalytic one of the individual.

'The inner world': the psychoanalytic mental state examination – historical background

This brief review contains some historical landmarks which are continually there in the back of my mind during everyday work as a psychiatrist. Freud started the ball rolling with the Schreber case, the examination of memoirs of a judge who recovered sufficiently to write about his psychotic experiences. In this paper, Freud described for the first time the process of projection, and the use of delusions in unsuccessful reparative efforts (Freud 1911). He also emphasised the central importance of narcissism in psychosis. Indeed, he called the psychoses the 'narcissistic neurosis' as he thought that psychotics were so self-centred that no transference occurred and therefore they were unanalysable (Freud 1914). At times, one can feel very sympathetic to this view.

It was some 50 years before Rosenfeld (1966) was to refute the notion of the absent transference in psychosis. Rosenfeld held that, far from being absent, the psychotic transference was of a concrete form. This view reinforced Segal's description of the concrete use of symbolism in the psychotic, in her terms a 'symbolic equation' in contrast to symbolism proper (Segal 1957). An example of the concreteness of the psychotic transference is where a patient hits a nurse for no apparent reason, concretely experiencing her as a persecutory parental figure. Another common example would be a patient who becomes persecuted by the newsreader on the television, and so smashes the screen.

An amusing example of concrete symbolism was a situation where a young schizophrenic took to banging all the doors at home. His father, also schizophrenic, dealt with the problem by removing the doors, including the front and back doors! One was left feeling sympathy for his wife having to cope with both her son's and husband's psychosis.

Prior to Rosenfeld's contribution, Melanie Klein had introduced some fundamental concepts. She held that the psychopathology of schizophrenia originated in the paranoid–schizoid position, with the leading affect being persecutory anxiety and the leading defence mechanisms splitting and projection. She emphasised the central importance of envy and the function of manic defence against intolerable confusion or depression (Segal 1973). O'Shaughnessy described how Klein approaches psychosis via anxiety, and that our earliest anxieties are psychotic in content. If the infant is unable to bind, work through and modify primitive anxieties, and terrifying figures that threaten to dominate the psyche, then the ego is driven to excessive use of otherwise normal defences of splitting and projective identification (O'Shaughnessy 1992). Thus Klein viewed psychosis in terms of an excessive use of normal defence mechanisms in relation to primitive anxieties. Later analysts developed further Freud's concept of narcissism in relation to the psychopathology of both borderline and psychotic disorders. Rosenfeld described how narcissism can become organised like a controlling gang, such as the Mafia, and he termed this destructive narcissism (Rosenfeld 1971). Sohn described how, through the formation of the narcissistic indentificate, narcissism can function in a highly organised negating manner in schizophrenia, accounting for Freud's despair of contact (Sohn 1985). I have described elsewhere how a schizophrenic patient in analysis went through a phrase where all sessional content was manipulated in such a triumphantly negating way (Lucas 1992).

Psychoanalytic models of psychosis

I am aware that the models I am presenting are gross over-simplifications of the complexities of the analytic contributions on the subject. However, the models serve to highlight differences of approach in a way that makes them accessible for comprehension and application by those of us working in general psychiatry. Analytic models of psychosis can broadly be divided into three groups.

1   General sensitivity approach

Following years of experience of intensive psychotherapy with schizophrenic patients at Chestnut Lodge, in the USA, Frieda Fromm-Reichmann, wrote: '...It is my belief that the problems and emotional difficulties of mental patients, neurotics or psychotics, are in principle to one another and also the emotional difficulties in living from which we all suffer at times' (Fromm-Reichmann 1960). More recently, another leading American, Giovacchini, shared this view. He wrote: '...In conclusion, difficulties in the treatment of psychotic patients do not derive so much from the contents of the patients' psychopathology as they stem from the analysts' sensitivities'. He added that 'being aware of their sensitivities, the countertransference broadens the range of patients we can treat' (Giovacchini 1979). While we need to be sensitive to all our patients, as human beings, there is a real danger in taking every communication on the same wavelength. If one ignores the psychopathology, ie what is meant by psychosis, we might be talking on wavelength 1, the normal or neurotic level, while the patient might be operating on wavelength 1,000 – an entirely different radio frequency (Lucas 1993). In other words, a caring attitude, while essential, is alone not enough.

2   The continuum model

A group of analysts subscribe to the view of a continuum model from neurosis to psychosis. This has been well summarised by Yorke (1991). Last century Hughlings Jackson talked of negative symptoms, as the result of loss of functioning caused by an illness and positive symptoms, as being related to attempts at recovery. Applying this model to psychosis the loss of ego functions leads to negative symptoms (object de-cathexis) while the phase of restitution leads to positive symptoms, *ie* hallucinations and delusions.

Yorke argues for a continuum between neuroses and psychoses, referring to two phases: (i) the pre-psychotic phase – dominated by regression and return of repressed material, similar to the clinical presentation of neurotic conflicts; (ii) the psychotic phase – dissolution of the ego, under the sway of the primary process, producing negative withdrawal symptoms, and the positive symptoms (hallucinations and delusions). Out of concern to place psychotic disorders within the existing framework of classical metapsychology, Yorke concluded: '...Indeed it is the fact that comparable conflicts are to be found in neuroses and psychoses, that has made the continuum theory so attractive to so many analysts' (Yorke 1991).

However, theories should not primarily be accepted on the grounds of fitting in with one's familiar way of viewing things. It might then be like asking a psychotic to fit into our preconceptions. Under stress, regression can bring about a fragmented, thought-disordered state. In Kleinian terms, this would be equivalent to regressing from the depressive to the paranoid–schizoid position. Using the continuum model, schizo-affective states of mind could be seen as regressive states, together with a temporary fragmentation, under stress, of the ego. Many patients might exhibit psychotic states under stress, especially those with borderline conditions. However, psychotic 'processes' need to be distinguished from major psychotic 'disorders', where, early on in life, psychopathology is already firmly established. Here a different approach to understanding might be needed.

3 Bion's model of differentiation

Bion introduced a quite new way of looking at psychosis. His theory resulted from detailed psychoanalytic studies of individual schizophrenic patients. Bion distinguished between the psychotic and non-psychotic parts of the personality. They function quite differently – the fundamental issue being how we cope with psychic pain. If we can tolerate frustrations, experiences not quite matching our preconception, then we can 'learn from experience' through bringing thinking to bear on the situation.

The psychotic part of the personality cannot learn from experience. Intolerant of psychic pain and frustration, the psychotic part uses the mind as a muscular organ to evacuate feelings and the part of the mind that registers them. If the feelings were verbal in origin, then the projection forms an auditory hallucination. If the feelings were evacuated through the eyes, then visual hallucinations result. If feelings (developed by the non-psychotic part) are concretely projected in surrounding external objects, they form 'bizarre objects'. In this situation, no distinction is made between the projection and the object.

It should be noted that general psychiatrists rarely ask how, psychodynamically, hallucinations are formed, *ie* they describe the patient hearing voices, but not how this has occurred. To my mind, Bion excitingly and convincingly demonstrated the process of genesis of hallucinations. You can see from this that psychoanalysis, in fact, has enormous contributions to make to the understanding of psychotic processes in modern-day psychiatry – and this knowledge is still vastly under-utilised. Having evacuated the emotional feelings, and the part of the mind that registered them, Bion pointed out that the psychotic part is left with only logical thinking to deal with emotional problems (Bion 1967).

The following serves as an amusing vignette of logical thinking. A chronic schizophrenic decided he wanted to leave hospital and wanted sex, so he wrote to the YWCA asking for a place there. He signed the letter 'Mr X, educated to A level standard, the world's best logician.' I received an irate phone call from the head of the YWCA asking me to speak with the patient and telling me that they were a single-gender hostel and that she was not amused. When I spoke to the patient, he said with no trace of emotion: 'I can't see the problem; if I went there it would be a mixed hostel.' Clearly his logic was impeccable, but there was something missing!

If the evacuation does not totally succeed, some in-touchness with psychic reality remains. Attempts are made to override this by adopting very moralistic omnipotent and omniscient attitudes. It is very common to see schizophrenic patients try to identify with religious absolutism. However, often they do not quite succeed. One patient who had converted from Christianity to Islam wanted our guidance as to exactly the right direction to point towards to Mecca in order to pray. Another patient complained that he had not totally been immersed in the holy water when baptised and felt an ankle remained vulnerable, like Achilles.

It is very common for a psychotic patient to use the defence mechanisms of denial and rationalisation. This leads to the psychiatrist doubting his own feelings and experiences – a familiar counter-transference experience. As Bion put it, he had an advantage listening to Hitler on the radio before the war, because he understood no German. As a result, he knew that he was listening to the rantings of a madman, rather than in danger of being seduced by propaganda. I share O'Shaughnessy's summary (1992) of Bion's contribution to psychosis:

> These are Bion's ideas. For me, they are that truly rare thing – new scientific ideas. They have thrown light on the obscure territory of psychosis, and they will, I feel for sure, illuminate it still further in the future.

The clinical cases will illustrate just how helpful are his ideas in trying to understand psychotic functioning. However, before that, I will briefly describe the structure and functioning of the day hospital.

The structure and functioning of the day hospital

The psychiatric day hospital comprised about 40 patients. The majority of patients suffered from major psychotic disorders, *ie* affective psychosis or schizophrenia. Some attended for the first time following a period of in-patient care. A substantial number were young schizophrenics. The nursing sister acted as the unit manager and co-ordinator of referrals. Three general psychiatrists shared the use of the day hospital, working in small teams with a clinical assistant, nurse and occupational therapist. In addition to the weekly team reviews, there were many other meetings, including self-run staff support groups and administrative meetings.

There were many form of therapeutic groups run by the occupational therapists and nurses. The types of groups varied depending on the skills and interests of the group leaders. In addition, there was some individual therapy (again the amount varies with staff resources and interests). Tensions could arise from staff shortages, interdisciplinary rivalries over who was in charge (*eg* occupational therapists or nurses with regard to a particular programme), and a continual threat that the day hospital could be resited with job losses. Within this setting, it was most important to foster an atmosphere in which each staff member was made to feel an equal, in that their opinion was encouraged, heard and respected. The day hospital sister occupied a key position. She was not attached to one particular team, but offered an overall counselling, supervision and monitoring role. As she put it, 'if the staff relationship is good, then so too will be the clients relationship'.

It was within this context that I ran a weekly, analytically orientated, supervision seminar. It was an hourly meeting to which all staff were invited to attend, as well as interested outsiders, for example the CPNs. It provided an opportunity for anyone to present a problem patient, whether or not that patient was being seen for individual therapy. It was an informal meeting where everyone was encouraged to be involved, and to express their opinion. Its aim was to foster a deeper understanding of the patient's psychopathology. The emphasis was to encourage all staff to utilise their particular interests and abilities to the maximum. I recall Robin Skynner once saying that there was no right way to run a group, *ie* there was not a textbook description that you could read, and then follow. I think the same applies to the management of psychotic patients. We must be flexible and mutually supportive in our approach to presenting problems. My aim in providing analytic perspectives through the weekly seminars is to encourage individuals in what was often difficult and challenging work, as illustrated in the following clinical examples.

Clinical examples

Case 1 – a patient for the day hospital

Miss C was a 19-year-old girl, who I saw for the first time in my out-patient clinic. She was brought by her elder sister. She showed florid features of schizophrenia. She presented with a smile, vague and child-like in manner; she was totally preoccupied with voices in her head from the Devil, telling her not to worship Jehovah. She felt that the Devil had put poison in her coffee, and linked this with a person bringing Jesus pictures to her mother when she was aged three. She was laughing while saying this, just like the old textbook description of the hebephrenic schizophrenic. Any attempt to make sense of it all left me with a headache (the counter-transferential consequence of trying to listen to a schizophrenic who is 'tearing your mind to pieces'). I just felt a continual despair. Where does one start with a patient like this, with a feeling of so little resources in the patient on which to call? Four weeks previously, she had set fire to the flat in which she lived with her father. She had the delusional experience that her aunt from abroad had come round at the instigation of her grandmother and was telling her to flick lighted matches into the bin in the kitchen. She did this and then went to have a bath, not realising that a fire might result. She subsequently had to escape via the balcony. At the time of flicking the matches, she saw the bin as her father's head. After the fire, her father moved temporarily into a one-bedroom flat, until this flat was renovated, while Miss C stayed at her sister's. There, she continued to behave irrationally, for example at times hitting her three-year-old niece for no apparent reason.

Her background history was that her family came from a foreign country, where her mother now lived. When Miss C was three, her mother had a schizophrenic breakdown. Miss C and her sister were sent back with the mother to the mother's country of origin. Six years later, they returned to live with the father, after her sister had written to her father threatening suicide if he did not bring them back. The report was that the mother had remained in a chronic psychotic state with persistent paranoid delusions. Since returning to England Miss C had relied totally on her older sister for thinking and guidance. Her father just ignored them emotionally.

Two years ago, her sister left home to live with her boyfriend. She was concerned for Miss C but soon had her hands full with her own baby. Miss C spend the next two years (until her breakdown) at home studying for two GCSEs. She attended a college sporadically and did not succeed in taking them. She has persistently presented her desire to study as a main concern. It is not uncommon for a schizophrenic from abroad, if there is a cultural emphasis on the importance of study, to use it as the answer for all life's problems in an unrealistic way. It is also not unusual for a young schizophrenic to have kept themselves together throughout childhood by reliance mentally on a sibling, using massive projective identification when the parents are unavailable for their emotional needs. When in adolescence they separate from the sibling, the breakdown occurs, as is illustrated in this patient's history.

We admitted her to hospital to further assess the situation. We saw the father, who confirmed the sister's picture of lack of involvement. He said that he had just left Miss C to get on with her studies over the last two years and had not noticed anything untoward. He seemed to fill his own time with work during the day, and drinking at home at night.

In hospital, with time and medication, the delusional experiences receded. Miss C remained with a vacant smile, child-like and talking unrealistically of returning to her studies. She was intending to return to live with her father once the flat was ready. The ward staff did not feel optimistic about getting anywhere with her. My view was that here was a young schizophrenic, at the start of life, seemingly with few internal resources of support, and that all she could do was to project everything out and then live in a dream world (the vacant smile). She needed a long period in the right environment, involved with caring professionals, not with isolated, unrealistic studying. My plan was for her to attend our psychiatric day hospital. I firmly told Miss C that what she needed at this point was time spent mixing with others in a helpful environment to develop more of a sense of herself, not studies. Her college had contacted me and I told her that they were in full agreement. There is a need to be firm in standing up to the psychotic part of the patient with its plans, though it will always try to change things back, ie make studying all that matters. The only straw of comfort to me, and evidence of life in her, was the fire. It symbolised her attempt to draw attention to her needs from her unresponsive father.

When she started at the day hospital, she remained vacant, smiling and child-like. As with the in-patient staff, the day hospital staff felt unable to make any meaningful contact with her. A few days later, on leaving the day hospital, she met a man when his car stopped at the traffic lights. She tapped on the window, got in his car and spent the night with him. The next morning, she was tearful and upset, telling the day staff about it. She then reverted to her vacant, smiling state. The staff felt at a loss, so the case was presented for detailed discussion at our weekly seminar.

The issue raised was that the patient appeared vacant and inaccessible, with nothing to get hold of, so it seemed hopeless. However, if one approaches from the psychotic wavelength, it looks quite different. We have a girl who uses projective processes to empty her mind of problems. In Bion's terms, the removal of the persecutory breast gives the same emotional satisfaction as having had a good feed, ie she gets the same satisfaction ridding her mind of her problems as if she had been able to think them through. Having emptied her mind of her problems, she is then free to produce any phantasy she likes. Here the phantasy produced by the man in the car is of an idealised phallus, like a sugar daddy, which would totally look after her needs. On returning to the day hospital after spending the night with the man, she initially had a smile all over her face, conveying a feeling of a child who was sucking her favourite lolly. Later, however, she started to feel uncomfortable and distressed about the past night's events. I felt that rapport with her could only be gained through our understanding involvement with the acting-out events and major life events that have impinged on her. As all that she can do at present is to evacuate and go vacant, we need to do the initial thinking for her about the projections. We had to do the thinking for the patient, like a mother for her baby, in Bion's terms through maternal reverie (Bion 1967) or in Winnicott's terms through a state of primary maternal preoccupation (Winnicott 1963, p.85) So instead of apparently nothing to take up with her we have:

(a) the unavailable ill mother;

(b) the relied-upon sister who left the need to resort to massive projection and hallucinating up her aunt, to try to make contact with father's mind;

(d) the issue of trying to use education and study to solve her emotional problems;

(e) the proneness to evacuate and look for quick ideal solutions, the sugar-daddy man/phallus, in preference to real involvement in the day hospital.

So what may appear arid from an ordinary viewpoint, looked at from the angle of dealing with a psychotic patient, is full of life events with which to be involved. It is possible to help staff to orientate themselves to this. They also need to realise that the patient will keep resorting to projection and escapism, and needs continually to be bought back to facing reality. After the seminar, one of our nursing staff was sufficiently encouraged to take the patient on for individual sessions. Also with the support from her sister (she would not move without her sister's agreement), her move to a specialised psychiatric hostel was arranged, while she would still continue to attend the day hospital.

Bion (1967) talked of the never-decided conflict between the life and the death instinct in the schizophrenic – the fight between the non-psychotic part that stays with frustrations with support from the therapist and others, and the psychotic part that evacuates and substitutes a delusional make-believe world in its place. If you are dealing with a psychotic patient, you must expect to be up against these opposing forces continually fluctuating.

With this patient, a few weeks later, she was talking of going abroad to visit her mother. Superficially this might sound normal, but looked at as a psychotic projective process it meant that she had disowned her needy state of mind into her mother. Then, it is as if she is free to deal with the problems now located in her mother in a quick, magical, manic way. She again had to be rescued back from that state of mind to reality. This happened. Then, off she went again, this time with a boyfriend from abroad, also suffering with schizophrenia, and who was also using endless studying to escape from reality. Again, she disowned her own problems *into* him; then she felt free to love him as the wished-for phantasy, caring boyfriend. Unfortunately, in reality he was more interested in any money she had than in her, and she felt very hurt and abused, and subsequently took an overdose. She took the overdose at a weekend and came back to the day hospital on the Monday as if nothing had happened. The therapist only learned about the overdose through a phone call from the casualty officer. Clearly, the omnipotent psychotic part of the patient's personality wished to split off its way of behaving from scrutiny.

As her omnipotent defences failed, she resorted to splitting her feelings into hearing voices of the angel and the Devil, but she was confused as to which people around her were the good ones and which the bad. If the therapist was experienced as standing for sanity and spoiling the dream world with the boyfriend, then she would be felt to be the voice of the Devil. On the other hand, if she was felt to be caring while telling home truths, she would be the angel.

One can see how being involved with these dynamics makes one consider what is going on when a patient talks like this, rather than just reaching for more tablets. Miss C had moved from her father's home to the hostel, but the hostel had staff problems and became less supportive, *eg* letting her stay in bed, rather than encourage her to attend the day hospital, saying that she was an adult and fit to decide for herself. Also, problems arose with the boyfriend. Finally her therapist was having to leave to have a baby, repeating the trauma of when her sister left.

With this background stress, she came back after a weekend to the day hospital and complained of voices telling her to go in front of the traffic. She was frightened. I have found that when a schizophrenic patient presents in a frightened state, it might be an indication that the psychotic personality is threatening to murderously attack the weaker, needy non-psychotic part, and this part is trying to communicate to receive help.

Two related examples spring to mind: one of a schizophrenic patient who jumped out of a window, but on detailed review in fact the needy part was pushed out by the psychotic personality (Lucas 1992); another of a schizophrenic patient who asked for admission, saying she was going to explode. Objectively there was no external evidence of it. We admitted her and in 24 hours she needed to be contained in the locked ward. On a previous admission she had drawn a picture of a volcano exploding. In other words, we need to be very sensitive to psychotic patients' communications when they say that they are frightened, and to support the fragile healthy part's needs and wishes.

With regard to Miss C we admitted her for a short while. During this time, we worked on her confusion between the angels and the devils. We talked with her about the hostel, the boyfriend and the therapist leaving, but that the day hospital, myself and the staff overall remained for her. Her confusional state receded and she returned to attend the day hospital.

Miss C's case, I think, illustrates the ever-shifting dynamics (between the life and death instincts) that inevitably one will come across with such patients. However, the case also shows that, using analytic insights, meaningful contact can be made with what initially appears as seemingly inaccessible.

Case 2 – finding the patient's 'wavelength'

This patient shows many features like those of the first one. Briefly, he presented as a 17-year-old adolescent. On leaving school, he joined the army, but after a while left following an ankle injury. He had a series of psychiatric admissions, presenting in a vague state, having been isolated at home. He was preoccupied with a (probably delusional) homosexual relationship in the army. Though he had several admissions he would not maintain attendance at the day hospital in between them.

Clinically he always presented smiling, with no eye contact, little speech, just staring disconcertingly into mid-space above one's head. I met both parents. I was struck by how the mother's mind was a blank in terms of any thinking about her son's emotional problems. After one admission, he was transferred to the hospital rehabilitation unit. After a while, he suddenly took himself home. A few months later, after he suddenly started to bang his head against the kitchen wall, his mother notified the GP and I was asked to do a domiciliary visit. On the visit, I was struck by an apparent lack of curiosity or questioning by his mother in relation to her son's recent disturbed behaviour. I was left wondering about having to rely on such a mother for the development of one's capacities for thinking and coping with emotions.

His father was very literal in his approach. He did not see him as ill, but lazy, though he had tried to help him to get a job. Therefore during a quick psychoanalytical mental state assessment one thinks that first he has a non-questioning mother and the alternative on offer is a somewhat self-centred, macho-like, literally minded father figure. So what is he to do when he reaches adolescence with the problems of achieving emotional separateness?

When he reaches adolescence the non-psychotic part is frail and underdeveloped. The psychotic part projects this awareness of his state into mid-space, and identifies with the macho father figure. He joins the army. When he can no longer live up to the army image, he breaks down and returns home. However, where is he mentally when he ignores ordinary contact and stares into mid-space? By accident, we found the answer. My junior doctor was rung by the head of a leading body-building organisation. My patient had written to him three times, asking if he would teach him to look like him. He offered himself homosexually in payment. The man wanted to reply to the letter in a helpful way, but added in a puzzled voice, 'But I'm not like that'. The man could not understand it – he was trying to use his ordinary sensitivities (*viz.* the sensitivity model). From the continuum model, one might view the situation as a disintegration of the ego under the sexual stresses of adolescence, but this theory misses out something, how to make contact with the patient and his smiling state.

In Bion's terms, we can now see how the psychotic part was operating. It had a smile on its face, like the cat that had got the cream – for it had its own answer to life's problems. It disowned the non-psychotic, thinking part of itself that had registered anxieties and comes up with its own solution, *ie* the homosexual identification with the body-builder.

It is interesting to recall how, in the Schreber case, Freud explained paranoia in terms of a defence against repressed passive homosexuality. The purpose of the externally projected passive homosexuality as a manic solution was evident in our patient. However, with the knowledge of where the patient's mind was, we could now take up with him his magical solution as an attempt to avoid psychic pain, and its recurring failure. We were now in a stronger position in offering the alternative of attendance at the day hospital, though, of course, a protracted struggle lay ahead, He then, in fact, started attending regularly for the first time, though he still stared ahead, making the staff feel that he was there in body, but not in mind. Still we felt that it was a start that his body was there!

Conclusion

In this paper, a case has been made for the central importance of psychoanalytic concepts in helping a group of staff working with the most difficult of patients in a day hospital setting. I personally only had two supervisions with Bion, shortly before he died. When I said how much I admired his work, he replied that 'the fun starts when you go off and do your own thing'. I think that we should be encouraged through his insights to feel free to utilise them in a flexible way when finding ourselves sharing challenging situations posed by patients in psychotic states of mind.

References

BION, W R (1967) *Second Thoughts: selected papers on psychoanalysis,* Maresfield Reprints, 1984. Chapters on 'Differentiation of the psychotic from non-psychotic personalities', 'Hallucination' and 'A theory of thinking'

FAHY, T & DAVID, A (1993) *Schizophrenia Monitor,* 3(1), p.8

FREUD, S (1911) 'Psycho-analytic notes on an autobiographical account of a case of paranoia (Dementia Paranoides)', S.E.12

—— (1914) *On Narcissism: an introduction,* S.E.14

FROMM-REICHMANN, F (1960) *Principles of Intensive Psychotherapy,* Chicago: University of Chicago Press

GELDER, M, GATH, D, & MAYOU, R (1990) *Oxford Textbook of Psychiatry,* Oxford: Oxford University Press

GIOVACCHINI, P L (1979) *The Treatment of Primitive Mental States,* New York & London: Jason Aronson, esp. pp.397–438

JONES, M (1952) *Social Psychiatry: a study of therapeutic communities*, Tavistock

LUCAS, R N (1992) 'The psychotic personality: a psychoanalytical theory and its application in clinical practices', *Psychoanalytic Psychotherapy*, 6(1), pp.3–17

—— (1993) 'The psychotic wavelength', *Psychoanalytic Psychotherapy*, 7(1), pp.15–24

O'SHAUGHNESSY, E (1992) 'Psychosis: not thinking in a bizarre world, in R Anderson (ed.) *Clinical Lectures on Klein and Bion'*, The New Library of Psychoanalysis no.14, Tavistock/Routledge, pp.89–101

ROSENFELD, H (1966) *Psychotic States: a psycho-analytical approach*, New York: Int. University Press

—— (1971) 'A clinical approach to the psychoanalytic theory of the life and death instincts: an investigation into the aggressive aspects of narcissism', *Psychoanalytic Psychotherapy*, 52, pp.169–78

SEGAL, H (1957) 'Notes on symbol formation', *International Journal of Psycho-Analysis*, 38, pp.391–7

—— (1973) *Introduction to the Work of Melanie Klein*, Hogarth Press

SOHN, L (1985) 'Narcissistic organisation, projective identifications and the formation of the identificate', *International Journal of Psycho-Analysis*, 66, pp.201–14

WINNICOTT, D W (1963) 'From dependence towards independence in the development of the individual' in *The Maturational Process and the Facilitating Environment*, Hogarth Press and the Institute of Psycho-Analysis, 1965

YORKE, C (1991) 'Freud's "On Narcissism: a teaching text"' in J Sandler *et al.* (eds), *Freud's 'On Narcissism: an introduction'*, Yale: Yale University Press, pp.35–53

6

David Bell

Destructive narcissism and *The Singing Detective*

The great neurologist, Hughlings Jackson, who much impressed Freud, once said: '...Find out all about dreams and you'll find out all about psychosis'. The world of our dreams is also, of course, the territory of artists. Works of art grip us in a profound way because they deal with unconscious concerns that are fundamental to us.

The television drama *The Singing Detective,* by Dennis Potter, is one such work. It deals with the tyranny of arrogance and cynicism, the terror of dependency, humiliation and shame. These are issues for all of us, but it is, I believe, in the psychotic patient that they reach their greatest intensity and become literally matters of life and death. Potter's narrative is striking in its explicitness and in its understanding of the internal world with its interweaving of memory, fantasy and reality. In this paper I will offer one way of understanding Potter's drama and I will compare it with some clinical illustrations from psychotic and non-psychotic patients.

Psychoanalysis has been immeasurably enriched by the understanding that has emerged from work with very disturbed patients. It soon became apparent that the difficulties these patients bring, and in such a concrete way, are not confined to the severely disturbed but represent universal human problems. Melanie Klein's work on early infantile experience provided a framework for the understanding of such primitive mental states. Her analysands Segal, Rosenfeld and Bion analysed the first schizophrenic patients using ordinary analytic technique. This work has formed the basis for understanding schizophrenia and other psychotic states, and it has also made an important contribution to the understanding of less disturbed patients. For the purposes of this paper I will explore only one aspect of these contributions – namely, Herbert Rosenfeld's work on destructive narcissism.

Rosenfeld (1971) discovered in the psychotic patients he treated a basic conflict between a healthy, sane part of the patient which recognises ordinary human needs and dependency, and another part of the personality which overwhelms the patient's sanity. This aspect of the personality functions like a tyrannising internal persecutor of enormous power. It contemptuously mocks all ordinary human inadequacy and dependency, and seduces the patient into an omnipotent world where destructiveness is idealised. Rosenfeld noted how frequently in the dreams and associations of these patients there were references to gangs of delinquents or Mafia-like figures which terrorise the patient and demand absolute allegiance. They appear especially after some therapeutic progress has been made. Such patients see the psychoanalyst as someone who is trying to weaken their power and force them into subservience. They frequently advertise their superiority over the analyst and thereby undermine all creativity and work. I will suggest that Dennis Potter's *Singing Detective* may be understood as a dramatic representation of these processes.

Synopsis and discussion of the narrative

The drama is a masterly interweaving of a man's childhood memories which centre on the psychic catastrophe of his mother's adultery, which he witnessed, and her subsequent suicide; his current life as a crippled patient in a hospital ward; and an inner fantasy world where he is the central character in a detective story he is writing. Actors play a multiplicity of roles so that, for example, mother's lover (a childhood memory), Binney the spy (in the detective fantasy) and his wife's lover (in the imagined external current reality) are all played by the same actor. This device emphasises the interweaving of fantasy, memory and reality.

The story opens with Phillip Marlow – a detective story writer, not a detective – lying in a hospital bed crippled with psoriasis and psoriatic arthropathy. He is full of biting invective, both bitter and cynical. He is at times apparently unmoved by the scenes of degradation and death that surround him. Of the nurses, he says: 'Like all morons, they have a mania for order – they put everything where I can't get it. Do you know how many O-levels you have to fail to be a nurse?' On being told off for having put another [black] patient's life in danger:

DOCTOR   He could have died of a heart attack.
MARLOW   That would be one less then.
DOCTOR   One less what?
MARLOW   Immigrant, Sunshine.

This cynicism is only superficial and he sobs in terrible pain when Ali, who has been a friend to him, dies. With this tirade he keeps at bay the shame and humiliation of his own condition. This, however, sometimes breaks through to be greeted, as he sees it, by embarrassed and contemptuous looks from impatient doctors and nurses. When the pain becomes unbearable, he retreats into a fantasy world where he is a smooth, unruffled detective moving in an underworld of bars, prostitutes and spies. He expects corruption everywhere – and finds it everywhere. The plot oscillates between these fantasies and childhood memories. The latter include victimisation by cruel parental figures (school teachers) and a memory of himself, as a child, in a very disturbed state of mind, shitting on the teacher's desk. His tyrannical teacher was more than willing to accept that it was not Phillip Marlow, her star pupil, who committed this desecration, and believed him when he pinned the blame on the class fool, Mark Binney, the son of his mother's lover. He later learned, in one of the most painful and poignant scenes in the whole work, that Mark Binney ended up as a chronic psychiatric patient.

In his actual life situation he imagines Nicola, his wife, as a corrupt figure betraying him both sexually and by stealing his work. At times, it is not clear what is memory and what is fantasy, and this is, of course, quite deliberate. Marlow is helped to uncover his fantasies and face himself by a psychotherapist. Although this is a therapeutic endeavour, from Marlow's point of view, it is a game of cat and mouse, winner and loser. As Marlow improves, so the figures in his external world acquire a different quality – they seem more benign and helpful. Nicola is no longer seen as betraying him.

In the final episode Marlow is emerging from his crippled state. There is a recapitulation of the central memories and fantasies. Firstly, we see Phillip as a child up a tree, watching his mother's intercourse with her lover. This is immediately followed by the gloom of an underground platform, with its references both to his memories of confronting his mother with his knowledge of her adulterous liaison, and her subsequent suicide. This is followed by a scene of Phillip with his father. They are walking home through the woods hand-in-hand. We then return to the scene on the ward and, in a deeply symbolic moment, Marlow tries to walk unaided. He stands and shouts: 'Look at me, look at me, I did it, I walked, I can walk.' Nicola rushes towards him.

> NICOLA   Phillip – what are you doing!
> MARLOW [*smirking*] Walking. *But on his face are rivulets of sweat.*
> NICOLA   For heaven's sake, suppose you fall over Phillip, hold on to me, you're not ready for this.
> MARLOW   Hold on to *you*!
> *She looks at him wryly, understanding well the resonances of the question.*
> NICOLA   There aren't too many others around any more Phillip.
> *They seemed to study each other, his face was still wet.*
> MARLOW   Be-bop-a-loo-bop.
> NICOLA   Yes, but isn't it time you climbed down out of your tree?

Marlow says, slightly later, in a delighted tone: 'Nicola isn't in the river.' This is a reference to a dead body found in a river in the detective fantasy. It is the body of a prostitute, but it also represents the dead body of his mother. He now seems delighted that Nicola is not his mother and that she is alive.

Two mysterious men appear on the ward wearing trench coats and trilby hats. They are referred to anonymously as First Mysterious Man and Second Mysterious Man.

> FIRST MYSTERIOUS MAN Where are you going?
> MARLOW Home.
> SECOND MYSTERIOUS MAN But that's off the page innit?
> *First Mysterious Man uses the flat of his hand on Marlow's chest, pushing him back.*
> FIRST MYSTERIOUS MAN You're going nowhere Sunshine, not until we settle this.
> *Marlow looks around for help and can see none. He moistens his lips.*
> MARLOW Settle what?
> FIRST MYSTERIOUS MAN Who we are, what we are.
> SECOND MYSTERIOUS MAN That's right, that's absolutely right.
> *Suddenly they grab hard at Marlow's arm and he cries out.*

Potter has said elsewhere that the story is a metaphor for self-discovery, and in the opening episode, he uses a much-loved metaphor for such a journey – going underground. 'And so the man went down the hole like Alice. But there were no bunny rabbits down this hole – it was a rat hole.' We see a figure go down in a sleazy bar beneath a pavement:

> [*voice over*] Into the rat hole ... down, down – one thing you don't do when you find yourself down one of those [*a rat hole*] is underestimate the rats in residence.

It is a journey to confront the most unsavoury aspects of the self. Potter refers to the ward elsewhere in the script as a 'place in the mind'. Marlow says about this place (the ward): 'one thing about this place ... it strips away all the unimportant stuff like skin – like work, loyalty – like passion and belief.' He is, in this journey, conducting an examination of his life; the way in which a particular internal world has been built up full of mocking figures which are idealised and distort all perception. Marlow, in the earlier part of the plot, identifies with these figures. Although he needs this mental organisation to protect him from completely unmanageable mental pain, he pays a high price for the use of this defensive structure. It is a 'psychic retreat' (see Steiner 1983). There is no psychic movement, no development. External figures are not distinguishable from internal figures. His world is divided between helpless contemptible victims and sadistic omnipotent oppressors (the school teachers, the spies, pimps and prostitutes, his wife and, of course, the psychotherapist). When Marlow himself is identified with the omnipotent figure, the terror of becoming a contemptible victim is never far away.

The development of the plot reveals an increasing coherence in the fantasies as they are sorted out from memories and from external reality. This is accompanied by Marlow's increasing physical mobility (symbolically representing psychic mobility). Again he remembers himself as a child observing his mother, watching from high up in a tree, as she made love to her lover; the memory of confronting her in front of some soldiers on a train, and of her suicide. Is there a connection in these events? Did he betray her? Like Marlow we are left unsure. Towards the end, the last representation of the memory of the mother's suicide and the theme of betrayal is re-worked but there is the recovery of a helpful object who holds his hand and who sings in tune with him – the father taking him home. At the moment when Marlow tries to walk 'to go home' towards more helpful figures, when he is separating himself from the cruel organisation and ceasing to be identified with it, the anonymous men[1] violently threaten him, demand allegiance and accuse him of betrayal. I hope you can see how close this is to the description by Rosenfeld of the internal Mafia – an internal surveillance system. I think it is important that the anonymous men say that he can go nowhere until they have been named and identified. I would see this as meaning that these anonymous personifications of parts of the self have to be named, have to have their nature understood. They can't just be escaped by an act of will.

Such conflict between need and hatred of need is part of all of us, but to some of our patients it is a crippling disease. They are isolated up a tree looking down on any ordinary human concern.

Clinical illustration

I will now give a brief clinical illustration from a psychotic patient. Mr A was a hebephrenic schizophrenic patient. His mother committed suicide soon after he was born. He came regularly to his sessions and sat staring at me in a state of blissful mocking serenity, totally silent and apparently untroubled by the silence, whilst I felt intense disturbance and discomfort. Occasionally, he would giggle or respond to something I said with a patronising comment. He seemed to be self-sufficient narcissistic omnipotence personified. In one session, however, he appeared to be in a very disturbed state and needed to talk to me urgently. He let me into his world. He told me that he was in communication with a group of people who were part of an organisation called 'The Scientists'. They gave him 'advice' and promised him everlasting life. If he killed himself, he could live forever. All he had to do was trust them. They forbade him from speaking about them. They also told him that he should not speak to Dr Bell as Dr Bell was quite mad and trying to destroy him.

The fact that the patient had told me this was obviously of great importance as, at the point of telling me, he was differentiating himself from the organisation. He was no longer identified with it. It appeared that he wanted to get out of their grip. After this session the patient became acutely distressed and threatened to throw himself under a train. He felt in enormous danger as he had betrayed 'The

Scientists' and told their secrets. His suicidal impulses were based on a terror of 'The Scientists' but also on a painful state of confusion in which he was no longer sure, as he put it, 'who was mad and who was sane'.

So, in this situation, one can see in a very concrete form, some of the human dilemmas Potter is describing. 'The Scientists' are very similar to the raincoated threatening figures who appeared when Marlow started to acknowledge helpful objects in his life and use their support to leave his crippled state. For Marlow they were fantasies which dominated his thinking, but for my patient they were hallucinatory experiences.

It is possible to see similar processes, though not in such concrete form, in patients who are less ill, as I will now illustrate. Mrs B, a 45-year-old married woman with three children, comes into the consulting room, typically a minute or two late, and repeats a process that she has gone through many times before. She gives a performance which could be called 'See how un-anxious I am'. She smiles, says 'Hi' and lies down on the couch, propping herself up on one arm. She distractedly strokes her hair, flicks it up and lets it fall, seems contained and calm whilst I, her analyst, start to feel rather impatient and uncomfortable, perhaps like a needy baby being faced with a mother who is preening herself. I call this a 'performance' because things have progressed a bit in Mrs B's analysis and she has been able to tell me what happens on these occasions. She has been coming late for her sessions for some time. During the day she experiences a sense of interest in coming to her sessions – an enthusiasm for meeting me as someone benign and helpful – but by the time of the session, this situation has drastically altered. She gets drawn into a state in which she believes that I have 'got her where I want her' – needing me. I am seen as feeling triumphant at this arrangement. In this state she becomes convinced that to come on time for her session and wait for me in the waiting-room would be to submit to a humiliating defeat. As she put it, 'I don't see why I should wait in the waiting-room, or follow you down the corridor like a dutiful and trained dog.' She went on to tell me that she had felt momentarily anxious about being late as she came into the consulting room, but her main concern was not to allow me to see that anxiety. She feels as if there is someone watching who would sneer and mock any visible vulnerability. She props herself up on the couch to maintain a sense of feeling in control and, during the silence, she has a debate with herself (or one might say two aspects of herself were in debate with each other). She says to herself, 'I'll tell him that I'm feeling worried.' Then another part of her says, 'Why tell *him* that, you know it will only make him self-satisfied; that's just what he wants, etc.' She thinks of things to tell me, then decides what I will think about it, thinks of putting it another way so that I will not be given any evidence of her being, as she would put it, a 'wimp' or a 'prat'. This process goes on and on and on, and her chance of getting help increasingly fades away as she feels trapped by the sneering, contemptuous part of herself that overwhelms her and with which she becomes identified. Sometimes she sees this part of herself present in the me, thus viewed as triumphant and self-satisfied. At other times it is thought of as existing in an observer who sneers at both of us.

At a very early age Mrs B embarked on a campaign to 'always be the one on top'. She apparently cried for the first two years of her life and then quite suddenly stopped and, as she put it, it's as if she has been grown up ever since. Any overt display of emotion was felt to be a contemptible loss of control. She was locked in a battle of a very sado-masochistic kind with her father in which he always seemed to end up appearing to her as a pathetic and denigrated figure, mocked by herself in collusion with mother. In her teens and early twenties she had a succession of promiscuous relationships in which she discarded men with great facility. She became part of a group or gang of young women whose aim was 'never to be the one left in need'. These women, with whom she is increasingly less friendly, have commonly appeared in sessions as figures imagined to be sneering at her if she is admitting too much to me. This way of living, the desperation to locate humiliating needs in other people, seemed to serve her well for a while, although she was never without anxiety of a deeply persecuting kind. She feared that she would get her come-uppance in some catastrophic way. This is the price many such patients pay for being 'up a tree' – there is a long way to fall. She suffered, in the same year, a number of losses – her younger sister died and six months later, her father. There was little outward disturbance, especially over her father's very long and lingering death – 'I just wanted him to pack his bags and get on with it'. I was, however, later to discover a deep terror of being trapped with and by persecuting and dying objects. She developed catastrophic anxiety and multiple physical symptoms. She felt constantly in danger of dying; this was experienced as a terrifying triumphant revenge by those she had triumphed over and ultimately, of course, her parents.

She was caught in a dilemma: she desperately needed help but to seek it was felt as a devastating betrayal as she became, in her own eyes, a 'pathetic wimp'. Desperately, she sought physical diagnoses, but eventually she accepted that the problem was psychological, or rather accepted it enough to start treatment.

I have given some idea of her dilemma in the initial part of the analysis. She felt trapped in a terrifying world; she needed help but this was felt to be a devastating humiliation. She would talk of various panics and symptoms associated with fear of dying; these accounts were punctuated by her saying, in a quite different and rather sarcastic superior tone of voice, 'how peculiar'. It seemed to me that every time she presented herself as prey to any irrational or uncontrollable emotions and terrors, she became identified with an internal mother who looked at her and said mockingly – 'how peculiar'. She tried to draw me into this mockery of her disturbance and, at times, it felt as if the analysis was experienced by her not as a therapeutic endeavour but as an investigation to expose a crime which must be punished: the crime was being ill. In the initial phase of the analysis she would bring letters to sessions which were written at home and which contained long accounts of terrifying states experienced in the middle of the night, in which she feared she would die. She would hand these letters to me at the end of the session and rush out of the door. One might say she was not permitted to admit this desperate aspect of herself into the analysis but had, so to speak, to slip it under the door as a secret message so that the internal surveillance system (like the anonymous men that watch Marlow) doesn't know about it. This represents a desperate appeal from a part of the personality trapped by the inner organisation which demands total control. Whenever a thought occurred to her that she didn't understand, she would say, 'I don't know why I think that', in a tone of desperate confession. The 'confession' was that there was something she didn't know. The internal system demanded omnipotence, not knowledge. Like Marlow, she could only believe in relationships in which one was up and the other down. Although she was deeply affected by breaks in the analysis, which were accompanied by terror of sudden death, she felt that interpretations concerning this were deliberate attempts by me to force dependence onto her. She was later able to tell me that she believed that people became psychiatrists and psychoanalysts in order to avail themselves of the opportunity of surrounding themselves with weak, spineless, wimpish patients who depended upon them. They did this to boost their own morale. As is typical for such patients, and as with Marlow, she believed that everyone was the same. She felt that behind my psychoanalytic face I was hypocritically exploiting her for my own narcissistic glorification. She sometimes felt I was sitting and admiring my interpretations without any interest in her. One might imagine a paradigm of infancy in which the mother apparently offers her baby a feed but is really caught up in admiring her own breasts and maternal capacities, while dismissing the baby.

I hope it is clear, from what I have said, that this particular patient has already moved a bit in her analysis. She had let me know about the appalling state of her inner world; by telling me about these things she differentiates herself from the internal organisation that dominates her life, and so dis-identifies herself with it. However, as with Marlow, a period in which she turns towards me for help, and seems to benefit from it, is followed by a period of intense persecution and humiliation, which she can only cure herself of by forcing it into me, advertising how useless I am, how little I have done for her and attacking me with bitter cynicism. After such episodes, she becomes frightened and vulnerable, feeling she has destroyed her analyst and thus has no one left to depend upon.

After there had been a very useful piece of work in which she felt deeply understood, she arrived half-an-hour late for the next session.

She told me, with excitement, that she was late for her session because she had been doing things that were much more important. During the half-hour in which she had delayed leaving work, she had been investigating the work of one of her subordinates whose work she had discovered was inadequate. She had gathered people around herself and was mounting what appeared to be almost a criminal investigation. It seemed to me that the criminal was herself, who was felt to be subordinate and inadequate for having allowed herself to be helped by me. This 'inadequate' part of herself now, located in the subordinate at work, was being tyrannised by a Mafia-like organisation with which she had become identified. The patient frequently dreams of being pursued by evil forces and black clouds.

In one dream she was being pursued by football hooligans and came up against a brick wall: 'There was a rather small, pathetic yapping dog at my feet which I wrapped in a plastic bag and lobbed over a wall.'

The yapping dog seemed, at first, to be a representation of her analyst, pathetically yapping away at her ankles, trying to get some attention. However, at another level it represented an infantile part of herself, depicted as the pathetic, yapping, whining dog, which is then hooliganised by suffocation and crushed to death (you will recall how she felt that my calling her from the waiting-room was to be led like a pathetic dog on a lead). As I said, in the earlier part of the analysis, breaks were catastrophic events. Having destroyed her analyst, she was left alone, frightened and vulnerable to dangerous attacks. However, after some working through of this in the analysis, she managed the breaks with less terror.

In one session, shortly before a break, she had become deeply involved in her work, something that had been previously a considerable problem for her as she always found it so persecuting. By contrast, involvement with her work now brought her pleasure and relief from persecution. However, as she came to the session she felt in great danger and felt that I was going to punish her for not thinking about the break. It was as if a sane realisation that the analytic work had helped her preserve a good image of me inside her that can support her over the break was being hijacked by a mad part of the personality that makes her think that she has to continually do a thing called 'thinking about me' in order not to be persecuted. She then feels she will be punished for having got immersed in her work whilst not consciously thinking about me: in other words she will be punished for not having omnipotent control of her own thoughts. It is, I believe, very important for these patients to be helped to distinguish sanity from madness, as very often they become confused, as here illustrated.

Before ending this section, I would like to briefly mention another patient in order to further show how important it is to help the patient make these distinctions between different parts of their personality which can become confused.

This is a patient who needed admission to hospital during her analysis. The transference was dominated by a relentless determination to possess me and never to be separated – to live inside me forever. Most unusually, she had made some important steps in getting herself looked after in preparation for a break; she had mobilised resources to support her, which meant to her co-operating with me and allowing me to have a holiday. After an empty silence, following some discussion of her arrangements for the break, she said, apparently out of the blue, 'I don't think I want you to know that I need you.' I was puzzled as her overwhelming need was not something that she tended to hide. I asked what had happened that had led her to say this. She told me that she had been having a fantasy of herself on a psychiatric ward being terrorised by a violent patient who had turned on her and pinned her to the floor. In the fantasy P, a nurse, asked if she was OK and she replies that she was 'alright'.

This material illustrates a difficulty one is constantly faced with in such patients: when co-operating and feeling helped in a realistic sense, she was overpowered by a ruthless violent part of herself (the violent patient) against whom she felt helpless and which silences her wish to obtain help. It illustrates how important it is that the analyst be active in getting access to the silenced needy part of the patient and is not bought off by the propaganda that everything is 'alright'. Further work in this session showed that the patient had told herself that if she told me she was frightened by the coming break and felt she needed me, I would accuse her of wanting to possess me and not permit me to have a holiday. In this sense, she was suggesting that I, not her, wouldn't be able to distinguish the sane, needy parts of herself from those aspects of herself that demand a mad, ruthless possession of me.

The representation of sexuality in *The Singing Detective*

I would now like to examine a related theme in the narrative that adds a further dimension, the representation of sexuality. Themes of violence and perverse sexuality feature prominently. The capacity to represent internally the parental couple in a loving and creative sexual act, occurring independently of the self's own wishes and desires, forms an important basis for creativity and psychological development.[2] In the drama, the central representation of the sexual act occurs when we see Phillip, the boy, up a tree looking down on his mother with her lover. Preceding this, he expresses his disgust of the natural world: staring at a beetle or ladybird his eyes narrow and he squashes it flat. He says, 'I can't abide things that creep and crawl and ... they got to be got rid of an', um? ... I can't abide dirt ... it'd get every-bloody-where, doan it?' Down below his branch, two human creatures are, so to speak, creeping and crawling, Philip's mother and her lover creeping through the undergrowth. Phillip observes them. The scene, the rhythmic movements of the couple, is interspersed with the now grown-up Phillip lying in a hospital bed, aghast, watching 'just as the boy watched' a man receiving cardiac massage, the same rhythmic movements. The sexual act, the supreme creative act of the parental couple, is suffused with horror, hatred, violence and disgust.

This scenario, a couple in intercourse and an observer, occurs repeatedly in the text as a prototype of human relations. The boy watching becomes the man on the ward who sees perverse relationships all around him. In his fantasy life, he has made this his profession – he is the detective who expects, finds and exposes the corrupt world that surrounds him. Sonia, a spy and prostitute, appears at one point in the detective fantasy making love with Binney the spy (another version of mother with Raymond, her lover). Later we see Marlow occupying the same position. He has just made love (or rather hate) with Sonia. There is a poignancy in this scene as he had remained dressed in order to conceal his psoriasis. I take this as representing, symbolically, his concealment of his vulnerability and feelings of humiliation, covering them over with hatred and cynicism.

MARLOW   I'm sorry, I ... look. It wasn't really me calling you names. I don't mean them. I don't want to do it ...
He turns and looks at the river [*dully*] The river looks as though it's made of tar, sludging along. Full of filth.

SONIA   What did you expect, Badedas?

The only view Marlow has obtainable to him of the sexual act then, is filth and sludge. This representation, or rather misrepresentation, of sexual intercourse is central to his psychopathology. Later in the text, Potter shows that lies about sex and mental illness are closely connected. Nicola has come to see him on the ward. He has progressed a little and they have the following conversation.

MARLOW   I'm going mad [*with precision*] I mean I'm going off my head. Round the bend. Bonkers. Losing my marbles. Cuckoo. Nuts. A candidate for the Funny Farm. Bananas is what I mean. Got it?

NICOLA   [*uneasy*] Do you want to talk about it or ... ?

MARLOW   Sex!

NICOLA   What?

MARLOW   That's what it's all about. Sex. Sex and lies.

In a moment of honesty, he recognises and affirms his longing. 'I want to sleep with you again.' Nicola is a bit taken aback. Marlow then turns his longing into a detailed perverse scenario in which he combines the sexual act with spitting at himself in a mirror. He says: '...Spitting at me, spitting at my own reflection. Couple of weeks ago my idea of happiness would have been to spit into your face.' His delight in the hatred of his objects has given way to an appalling disgust of himself. The fantasy of the mirror, of course, makes him able to occupy both positions, participant in and observer of, the perverse sexual act.

The psychotherapist who is attempting to help Marlow clearly sees the importance of this aspect of his character.

> DR GIBBON [*referring to one of Marlow's books*] There's a paragraph here that sits rather oddly on the page. It doesn't belong to the detective story – not in my opinion.
>
> MARLOW   Oh, I see. Psychiatry is not nasty enough for you. You still want to get into literary criticism, do you, running down the slope, with the swine to the left of you, swine to the right of you, grunt, grunt.
>
> DR GIBBON   Listen to this. A purple passage.
>
> MARLOW   No. A blue one, I hope.
>
> DR GIBBON   [*reads*] Mouth sucking wet and slack at mouth chafing limb thrusting upon limb, skin rubbing at skin.
>
> MARLOW   Oink, oink.
>
> DR GIBBON   Faces contort and stretch in helpless leer, organs spurt smelly stains and sticky betrayals. This is the sweaty farce out of which we are brought into being …

This sweaty farce then, is what has become, in his mind, of the parental sexual act. The same words, 'slack and wet', later refer to Noddy, the decrepit, drooling, cadaverous character in the next bed.

Potter, here, clearly identifies the link between a narcissistic character structure and this misrepresentation of the parental sexual act. This misrepresentation, a sort of internal lying, is poison to the mind.

I described earlier that as the narrative progresses, there is a transformation of these internal representations. At the end, Marlow leaves the ward with Nicola, now represented as warm and desirable and also more ordinarily human. As they walk out, he is leaning on her. Again, there is an observer, us, but also the dramatic device of Reginald who has been reading Marlow's detective novel throughout, and has just come to the last lines:

> 'And her soft red lips clamped themselves on his.'
> He closes the books and says, warmly, 'Lucky Devil.'
> [*ie* the couple are now admired.]

There are many patients who, like Marlow, cannot maintain an internal representation of a loving intercourse. It is attacked and denigrated by powerful internal forces linked to 'the Mafia'. Such patients, when they feel transiently able to engage enthusiastically with objects in their world or with their analyst, feel in great danger. They feel observed by terrifying forces felt to be external. In such situations, the sexual act is frequently represented mainly as either terrifyingly violent or is enviously degraded and becomes contemptible.

In a session not long before a break and following a session in which there had been some useful work concerning the terror of the coming separation, Mrs B talked of a dream of being left all alone with a murderous rapist. She said, at the beginning, *sotto voce*: 'I feel a bit better today (*quietly, tentatively*), It may have something to do with yesterday's session and ...'. Quite suddenly, this scenario, in which the two of us are viewed as involved in something good and useful, is turned into something very different. Her tone changed. She told me that she was telling herself: 'Oh well, if humiliation can help me get better, I'll humiliate myself. I'll grovel at your feet and tell you how wonderful you are.' There is thus now a view that it is not the valuable work that helped her, but only self-humiliation, a perverse twisting of reality. The good intercourse/feeding situation has been hijacked, partly as an expression of envy and partly out of terror of it. Who is watching us?

The final dénouement

Before ending, I would like to discuss, briefly, the ending of *The Singing Detective*, which I thought rather ambiguous. You remember that the Mysterious Men came into the ward at the point where Marlow moved towards Nicola, now viewed as a helpful supportive figure. What follows is a violent shoot-out. The 'Singing Detective' (a fantasy) bursts through the doors into the reality of the ward with his gun firing. He annihilates everyone on the ward: patients and nurses. Here fantasy and reality coalesce. Horrified, Marlow watches from his bed. As the 'Singing Detective' shoots the First Mysterious Man, Marlow says: 'Stop, it's murder.' The 'Singing Detective' replies, 'I'd call it pruning.' As the 'Singing Detective' aims at the Second Mysterious Man, he fires. But it is Marlow who gets the bullet in his forehead, thus showing that the Mysterious Men are part of Marlow's personality.

The ward then returns to normal and appears peaceful. Marlow is now better and able to leave the ward and exits arm-in-arm with Nicola. We hear Reginald, a fellow patient, read aloud from the novel *The Singing Detective*: ' ... and her soft red lips clamped themselves on his ... The end.'

Finally we hear Vera Lynn's famous war-time song, *We'll meet again*, and this, I think, can be taken as alluding to the recognition that the whole process will have to be gone through yet again, but hopefully next time on a more secure footing.

Conclusion

In this paper I have illustrated Rosenfeld's theory of destructive narcissism using Dennis Potter's TV drama, and clinical material from psychotic and non-psychotic patients. I have tried to show how the apparently bizarre world of a schizophrenic patient can be seen as a concrete manifestation of experiences that are common. When Freud attended to the delusional self-persecution of the melancholic patient, it led him to the discovery of the super-ego present in all of us. Rosenfeld's theory can be seen as an extension and careful phenomenological analysis of these archaic destructive processes. I also show the link between this type of narcissistic pathology and the misrepresentation of the sexual act. I have attempted to demonstrate a similarity between the processes involved in the development of Potter's drama and those involved in the process of psychoanalysis. Much of the work of analysis involves helping the patient distinguish between fantasy, memory and external reality. The development of the capacity to perceive the internal world, namely to have insight, is a precondition for being able to have a firm relation to external reality. Fundamental to this endeavour is the development of the ability to distinguish between the psychotic and non-psychotic parts of the personality[3] and to recognise things for what they really are. At the end of *The Singing Detective*, Marlow is not able to make his final move towards health until he can name the Mysterious Men.

In a television interview (see Fuller, 1993) Dennis Potter discussed the character of Philip Marlow and the structure of *The Singing Detective*. I think it could also be used as an analogy for some of the things that go on in any analysis. He said:

It is the [illness] that is the crisis ... it is the illness which has stripped him ... that starting point of extreme crisis and no belief, nothing except pain and a cry of hate out of which were assembled the fantasies and the fantasies became facts and the facts became memories and the memories became fantasies and the fantasies became realities and all of them become him and all of them allowed him to walk.

Of the structure of *The Singing Detective* he says:

By being able to use, say, the musical convention and the detective story convention and the 'autobiographical' convention, and making them coexist at the same time so that the past and present weren't in strict sequence, because they aren't – they are, in one sense, obviously in the calendar sense – but they're not in your head in that sequence and neither are they in terms of the way you discover things about yourself, where an event of 20 years ago can follow yesterday, instead of precede it ... out of the morass, if you like, of evidence, the clues and the searchings and strivings, which is the metaphor for the way we live, we can start to put up the structure called self. In that structure we can walk out of that structure and say at least now we know better who we are.

Notes

1 Who, we are told in the text, work for an 'intelligence organisation'.
2 Britton (1989) has shown the intrinsic links between the capacity to represent triangularity and the capacity to think about oneself.
3 See Bion (1967).

References

BION, W R (1967) 'Differentiation of the psychotic from the non-psychotic personalities' in *Second Thoughts: selected papers on psychoanalysis*, 1984

BRITTON, R (1989) 'The missing link' in R Britton, M Feldman & E O'Shaughnessy (eds) *The Oedipus Complex Today*, Karnac Books

FULLER, G (1993) *Potter on Potter*, Faber & Faber

ROSENFELD, A (1971) 'A clinical approach to the psychoanalytical theory of the life and death instincts: an investigation into the aggressive aspects of narcissism', *International Journal of Psycho-Analysis*, 52, pp.169–79, reprinted in E B Spillius (ed.) *Melanie Klein Today*, Vol.1, Routledge, 1990

STEINER, J (1993) *Psychic Retreats*, Routledge

Index